KITESURFING

THE COMPLETE GUIDE

Ian Currer
Foreword by Paul Jobin

Published by :

Lakes Paragliding, Greyber, Maulds Meaburn, Penrith, Cumbria, CA10 3HX, UK

© Lakes Paragliding 2002

This book is copyright under the Berne convention. All rights are reserved. Apart from any fair dealing for research, private study, or review as permitted under the Copyright Act 1956, no part of this publication may be reproduced, stored in a retrieval system, or transmitted in any form or by any means electronic, mechanical, photocopying, recording or otherwise, without the permission of the copyright holder.

British Library Cataloguing in Publishing Data

A catalogue record for this book is available from te British Library.

ISBN: 0-9542896-0-9

Text: Ian Currer

Illustrations: David Barber

Page design & layout: Neil Cruickshank

Printed and bound: Perfils, Spain

Front Cover Picture: *Courtesy of F-One Kitesurfing*

Contents

Acknowledgements

I would like to thank the following people and companies for their support in making this book possible.

Jeremy Pilkington & Flexifoil International Ltd.

Club Mistral, Safaga, Egypt

Mac Aviation

The BKSA.

John Thompson of the Kite Shack

Trevor Sargent at KiteboardingUK

Gus Hurst of f8 Photography

TKC Sales Ltd

Jacky Bevan

...other readers / proofers

And all those who advertised in it, sent in photos and encouraged and supported this project. You know who you are!

Foreword

Kitesurfing (also known as kiteboarding) is a sport that is not only expanding quickly but also constantly developing. Together with this rapid growth there are also many signs of maturity; for instance: the emergence of national associations, led by the British Kite Surfing Association (the worlds' largest); the setting up of organised training systems; and with this publication, a practical guide book and manual.

"Kitesurfing - The Complete Guide" is an invaluable reference, for those people who may be interested in taking up the sport, those already learning and those who are already accomplished riders.

Ian Currer has pulled together a host of information and lays it out in a logical manner. He discusses topics such as whether this is the sport for you, what equipment you may require and what you can expect from a training programme. This book offers insight into everything from the basics of choosing a suitable spot, right through to topics such as competitions and phenomena such as "apparent wind".

The text is clear and informative throughout and avoids technical jargon wherever possible. David Barber's illustrations are superb and do an excellent job of clarifying the topics covered in the book.

Ian, the author of Touching Cloudbase, the worlds' best selling manual on paragliding is the main architect of the British Hang-Gliding and Paragliding Association's training system. His 25 years expertise as an outdoor sports instructor is apparent in the way he breaks down each topic into manageable and easily understood sections, and his enthusiasm for Kitesurfing shines through in his writing.

This is not a "Do-It-Yourself" manual, but it will prove to be an enormous help to anyone who is learning, will give a useful insight into the sport for anyone thinking about having a go, and will act as a handy reference for more experienced riders too.

This book should be a vital component in every rider's outfit.

Paul Jobin, May 2002
Chairman: British Kite Surfing Association
info@kitesurfing.org
www.kitesurfing.org

1 Introduction

If you have started, or are thinking of starting kitesurfing, your visions of skimming the water and performing spectacular jumps could soon be reality. This newest of sports combines the speed and thrills of windsurfing with the radical tricks of wakeboarding and offers the potential for huge jumps even from flat water. The kit is comparatively small; there is no need for a boat, and it can be done in winds varying from just 8 or 10 knots right up to howling conditions.

Kitesurfing is relatively easy to learn. For those who already have windsurfing or wakeboarding skills it is possible to get blasting in just a few hours.

There will be many challenges of course, and it will take some time and effort and probably a few disappointments before you become a competent kitesurfer, but it will be worth it for the rare experience of being one of the few to master the newest and most exhilarating of sports.

This handbook is meant as an aid to learning, to be referred to before, during and after your training. It is not meant as a do-it-yourself manual. Kites are usually thought of as toys, but large traction kites are by nature very powerful and deserve considerable respect. Kitesurfing could result in injury or even death if practised incorrectly, especially if attempted in the wrong place or the wrong weather conditions. The only safe way to learn is to be trained by a competent instructor.

Occasionally in this book kitesurfers are referred to as "he": this is simply for the sake of writing style. Kitesurfing is of course a sport that can be equally well enjoyed by both men and women.

The sport is still young and rapid developments are taking place. To keep the information current, the publishers are maintaining a website of additions and updates at www.kitesurfUK.co.uk

Photo: F-One Kitesurfing

Julie Prochaska - one of the world's top female riders

A Brief History

Modern kite surfing may seem to have a shorter history than most sports, but its roots go back quite a way. For several thousand years the Chinese, in particular, have been flying kites. Legend has it that the first kite was invented by a farmer who tied a string to his hat to prevent him from losing it when it was blown off in the wind.

There is little doubt that man-lifting kites have been used for centuries; Marco Polo remarked that only a fool or a drunkard would allow himself to be lifted into the air by a kite, and this was in the thirteenth century! The power of a good-sized kite on a breezy day was clearly well understood. Perhaps these kites were used to power small watercraft, we do not know, but it is certain that the concept of body dragging is not a new invention!

Like many sports, kitesurfing evolved from a fusion of existing skills and equipment; water-skiing, windsurfing, parachuting and paragliding have all played their part, and of course kites themselves, as mentioned, have been around a very long time.

Benjamin Franklin, best known for his experiments in 1752 with kites and lightning, was also a great innovator and lover of kites as a youth, and he often tied a kite to his boat to get a free ride.

In 1825 George Pocock, an English schoolteacher, and some of his friends, travelled regularly in a carriage pulled by a stack of kites, on one occasion achieving a speed of 30 miles an hour.

In the early 60's several waterskiers began to hang on to large flat or Rogallo kites to fly behind their tow boats or do huge jumps. The rogallos were in fact the ancestors of modern hang-gliders. On breezy days these big kites were occasionally found to supply sufficient power for the skiers to keep moving without the boat.

A 17th Century British kite flyer!

Rogallo hang-glider 1976

Several pioneers also managed to power themselves - usually on water skis - using a stack of conventional kites; the "Jacobs ladder" approach, still popular with power kite flyers today.

Kite powered water craft also appealed to the less conventional sailors. Having been turned back by the coast guard from an Atlantic crossing attempt on his 16ft Hobie Cat, Don Eisaman of Michigan set out to cross the 5 great lakes in the US in his kite powered 8ft inflatable dinghy. (He has managed 4 at the time of writing!)

At the end of the sixties another development, the ram air-parachute, was transforming the skydiving world, with new rigs that actually flew like wings rather than just slowing the fall. In the early eighties, this technology was taken another step with the use of high- performance airfoils and new materials, and foot launched paragliders capable of soaring flight appeared.

The manufacturers of these wings made many refinements to the flexible airfoil and a good proportion are active today in producing high-performance kites for kitesurfing.

Ram-air foils were soon popular for recreational kites too, and unlike previous kite design that relied simply on drag, the new shapes used airfoil sections and generated lift as well, offering twice the power for the same area. Powerkiting was born, and spin-offs like buggies were quick to follow. Some kitesurfing was taking place already, as water was an obvious place to use the power of these wings. In 1988 Cory Moesler won the Johnnie Walker speed sailing championships for craft with a 10m sail or less. By using waterskis and a kite, he beat the next nearest competitor by a huge margin, demonstrating the inherent superiority of a moving kite to a static sail.

Of course there was already a group of sailors who had simple equipment and high speed as their main interests. It was not long before the windsurfing fraternity entered the picture...

Windsurfing is a highly popular sport that has been in existence for many years. Driven by both manufacturers and sailors, the sport has become increasingly technical, with performance advances becoming smaller each year.

Like some other sports the gulf between the experts and the beginners was growing ever larger. It is only comparatively recently that the focus has once again switched to making the sport user-friendly for a wider range of people.

A modern paraglider. (Photo: Gin Gliders)

Windsurfing is still not an easy sport to learn!

Although replacing the sail of a windsurfer with a kite seems fairly obvious, there are a number of practical problems. With no mast foot pressure the dynamics of the whole system are changed quite radically. The rider's weight must be moved forward towards the middle of the board, and even if the footstraps are moved to allow this, a windsurf board is often too large to sail easily with a kite.

However the appeal of a "new" wind-powered watersport to windsurfers is easy to see, particularly one that allows such a great potential for jumps and performance in lighter winds, and many of the skill are transferable.

What was needed was an application of the skills of windsurfers and kiting, together with the effort to overcome the technical problems of making kitesurfing a practical proposition. Fortunately for us, the Legaignoux brothers, based in the south of France, had the combination of skills and vision to overcome the difficulties and design the original Wipika kite, and with it the sport of kitesurfing as we know it.

There were a few problems to overcome. The first hurdle of finding a suitable board was solved quite easily, simply using existing surfboards or wakeboards with footstraps screwed into the appropriate positions. Another problem was simply controlling such a powerful kite without too much strain on the arms. The bar system was added together with a loop that could be "hooked into" with a windsurfing harness.

The greatest challenge, however, was re-launching the kite from the water. Both rigid "hang-glider" types and ram air kites have an unfortunate habit of remaining down once wet, either because part of the structure becomes submerged or because water gets inside the cells.

Perhaps the single most important development that made kitesurfing practical was the advent of the Legaignoux inflatable kite. Their early kites were single skinned with curved leading edges and inflatable spars making them impossible to submerge in all but the fiercest waves.

The shape prevented it from lying flat on the surface, and so given sufficient wind, the downed kite would easily drift to full line stretch position and re-launch without the problems of water in the cells. The lifting performance of this type of kite is relatively poor, but that is easily remedied simply by using a greater surface area, and the re-launchability

The Wipika Classic kite.

made it the easiest by far for the new kitesurfer to use. Finally, having produced a kite that will self launch, there is the problem of how to stop it dragging you forever if you should lose control! The introduction of leashes and quick release mechanisms took care of this final barrier.

All the elements were in place to enable kitesurfing to become a practical sport.

Needless to say there are now several companies using a variation on the inflatable spar design; many are licensed users of the Legaignoux patent and many more designers are working on producing different solutions to the re-launch problem.

Over the last few years, as the sport has grown, there has been an explosion of development in the equipment, the techniques and the standard of tuition available.

Twin tip and asymmetric boards, ram-air and high aspect ratio kites and professional schools have all come into being. The National association has grown rapidly and whilst it is still early days for the sport the future is looking good.

The sport first became popular in places such as the south of France & other Mediterranean beaches, Florida, Hawaii and other similar places. In fact wherever a significant section of the population is more interested in enjoying themselves than working. (Holiday resorts I mean of course). In the UK Kitesurfing is now practised on beaches throughout the country.

Windsurfers, wakeboarders, powerkiters and paraglider pilots have all been attracted into this new sport, and as its popularity grows it is surely inevitable that its appeal will spread and it will become a familiar sight on lakes and beaches throughout the world.

Getting Started

Kitesurfing is a great sport, but to ride safely and make good progress you will need training. This may be from other riders or from an instructor, which is strongly recommended. In either case this book is laid out in pretty much the order that the subjects and techniques will come up. Of course you may need to jump around and refer back to some chapters, but it is logical to start out with an overview of the likely training programme.

Before you even start kitesurfing you can help yourself a lot by becoming familiar with power kites in general. Students who have spent a few hours practicing with a traction kite are always better prepared and progress faster than those who start from scratch.

Kitesurfing can be fairly demanding to learn, so the best way is to break it down into manageable chunks and work at each skill before progressing to the next. It is very tempting to just buy all the gear and take yourself off to the nearest beach, but this method has a high failure rate!

Getting ready for some power kite flying, these 10ft kites are being stacked to form a "Jacobs ladder"; a technique used in the earliest attempts at kitesurfing. (Photo: Flexifoil)

The Training System

Different countries and different training operations will use slightly varying techniques and systems. This outline is intended as a general guide as to what you should expect. (If it is radically different it is worth asking why!)

A good course will always begin with students being warned of the dangers involved in a sport like Kitesurfing; a check should be made of their fitness and ability to swim, and everyone needs to sign up for public liability insurance. For obvious reasons a contact address and details need to be taken by the instructor before training commences. The school should provide helmets and buoyancy aids for pupils.

1. Choosing a good site & correct wind.

The site must be large enough to allow at least 3 line lengths downwind of the flying area without any obstruction. Sandy beaches are ideal, but grass or some other smooth surface that will not damage the kite is also suitable.

There must be no power lines, nearby airports or other dangerous hazards and the area should be well away from roads, so that an escaped kite will not cause anyone else a problem. It is critical that consideration is given to other people; an out of control kite can seriously injure a passer-by, and it is worth walking a long way to find an unpopulated bit of beach or field. If others do come near you the kite must always be secured before they get within range!

The wind should be a reasonable breeze, enough to allow you to feel the power when the kite is moving fast. If you cannot stand still with the kite in the safe position above you then the wind is too strong or the kite chosen is too big.

If the wind is light a full size traction kite may be used, but is more usual to start with a smaller kite, perhaps of 2 or 3 square metres.

2. An introduction to power kites.

The first job is to check the gear and learn how to set it up. This may include disentangling lines, pumping up inflatable kites and securing them with sand. Connecting the lines with lark's head knots, and the control bar and safety leash. Once the gear is ready the instructor will demonstrate how to launch the kite and control it using the bar. (It is assumed that most beginners will start with a 2 line kite for simplicity) Once demonstrated each student will have a turn at practising the launch and control technique.

3. The window and safe (zenith) position.

This will be explained and demonstrated.

HQ Nasa single surface traction kite, commonly used for training .
(Photo: f8 Photography)

4. Control exercises.

These will typically will be to fly the kite to the edge of the window and refine your control by touching the wingtip to the ground on each side. During this exercise the kite should be controlled slowly and smoothly, and the correct stance with feet together, knees flexed and straight arms should be mastered.

5. Working the kite and controlling power.

These exercises are to introduce the control patterns you will need on the water, doing vertical S patterns on one side of the window only, then moving on to horizontal S patterns through the central power band.

As you work the kite there may be enough force to drag you down the beach or field (this is why sand is best). A smooth pattern with constant power should result in a good straight consistent drag down the beach. (This is easily checked by looking at your heel tracks in the sand!) Smooth straight pulls at this stage will translate into long smooth rides on the board later, so it is worth practising now.

6. The emergency drop.

Inevitably at some point you will need to stop the kite, perhaps due to other water users or some other hazard, or just because you need to sort yourself out. Any reasonable two line kite will be fitted with a leash for your wrist that enables you to simply drop the bar and remain in contact with the kite as it flutters down.

7. Using the harness.

This exercise covers setting up and hooking into the harness and controlling the kite through the bar with one hand.

8. Putting it together.

You should now be able to launch the kite, hook in, fly it with one hand whilst you sit or squat down, attach a leash to one foot or your harness, stand up again, and, carrying a board in one hand, walk a few metres to the left or right or around a couple of obstacles. (You may very well just use a bag or other object rather than a real board for this exercise) The point is self-evident: practicing the technique you will need fix your leash, scoop up your board and enter the water.

9. Traction.

Once you can manage the exercise above quite well with the kite in a stationary position, it is worth practising being dragged in a big zig -zag whilst under power (ie working the kite in fast S turns on one side of the window, then the other.)

The Author gets in a bit of scudding practice!
(Photo: f8 Photography)

Practice using the wrist leash to drop the kite before getting in the water.
(Photo: f8Photgraphy)

If you can manage this you will have most of the flying skills you need to put together to kitesurf.

10. Theory.

You will be trained about the sectors of the window, how to increase and decrease power and where to place the kite for best effect in different situations (e.g Higher up for more down-wind beats), basic weather and site assessment.

11. Dry water starts

The final dry land exercise is to practise the start. Begin by sitting on the sand with both feet in front of you as if on a board. Unhook your harness, fly the kite to high in the back half of the window then turn it hard and dive it through the power band in the leading half of the window. This will pull you to your feet and start you moving. Reverse controls to stop it diving into the ground and go straight into a smooth "S" pattern in the front half of the window . This will keep you powered up and moving at an angle as in exercise 8. A helpful device for practicing the "swoop" start manoeuvre is a dummy board with footstraps (an old snowboard deck or similar) that you can use for footstrap location practice.

12. Body dragging.

Learning to control the kite in the water and get more practice at keeping the power delivery smooth. Further practice at controlling direction by using the window sectors.

13. Water re-launching techniques.

First standing, and then from a prone or supine position.

14. Introducing the board.

Learning how to handle the board in the water and how to get your feet into the board straps.

You will need a lot of launch practice.
(Photo: R Cruickshank)

15. Starting from the water and maintaining balance.

This will take quite a bit of practice, as you will now be trying to work the kite smoothly, maintain balance and foot steer the board, at the same time keeping a lookout ahead.

16. Controlling power, speed and direction.

Speed management and learning to edge the board to make progress upwind.

17. Self rescue and dealing with problems.

18. Turning.

You will learn how to switch direction, either by toe-down riding, using a twin tip board (if appropriate) or gybing with both the "early foot change and "late foot change" techniques.

19. Beach start.

The step on technique.

20. Using the de-power system.

21. Different kite types.

More advanced exercises include jumping, wake boards with bindings etc. These are generally not included in a training syllabus, but become more applicable with experience.

Putting it all together (Pic: f8 photography)

Introducing the board. (Photo: R Cruickshank)

Health & Safety

Kites and Kitesurfing exist for just one purpose; because they are fun.

However the power of these playthings is sufficient to cause injury or worse if they are misused and anyone wishing to use one must bear in mind a few simple safety considerations.

Health Considerations

Are you healthy enough to participate? If you are feeling unwell or are nursing a previous injury or have some problem that would prevent you from coping with being pulled over, or being dragged; then it is probably wise to give this a miss.

Once in the water you may quickly find yourself facing a long swim, and in wavy conditions you will certainly get a good ducking. Obviously being a strong swimmer and at home in the water is a definite prerequisite for a kitesurfer.

Medical conditions such as heart problems or diabetes may also be a hazard as your body will be subjected to a great deal of strain and your energy demands when hammering through rough water at 20 knots are extremely high! Perhaps the most problematical aspect for many people is the fact that unlike some sports, you cannot necessarily simply stop when you have had enough. Even if you are cold, tired and waterlogged you may still need to be able to summon the effort to sail or walk back to your start point.

Spot the hazards… you do need to be realistic about your abilities. (Photo: F-One Kitesurfing)

Do not ride in conditions that are too much for you.
(Photo: F-One Kitesurfing)

General Safety

Kite surfing can be easy; it can certainly look very easy, but do be realistic when deciding what you are capable of. It is better to be on the beach wishing you were out there, than out there wishing you were on the beach!

In practical terms you do need to be able to assess the weather situation, and whether your equipment is appropriate. This means the wind strength, the direction, the gustiness, and the state of the water. Like all watersports it is important that the kitesurfer is aware not only of the wave height and direction, but also the state of the tide and currents if sailing on the sea.

Water temperature and wind chill are other factors that will determine the safe limit of your time on the water.

There are further chapters in this book to help you make this kind of evaluation. The best recommendation how-

ever is to sail with other kitesurfers and take advice from those with the best local knowledge and experience. Never sail in poor visibility, whether caused by poor weather or by the onset of dusk; the risks of disorientation and collision are obviously magnified.

If you do choose to sail alone, ensure that there is always someone on land to keep an eye on you, and someone who knows how long you expect to be out

Understanding the Wind

Kitesurfing is only possible by harnessing the power of the wind, so in order to do it well it is important to understand a little about the wind and how it behaves. Will the wind increase later or change direction? Will the airflow be smooth or turbulent? Is there a spot that is better to launch?

How the air behaves is of crucial importance to us so we need to understand a bit about it and its behaviour in order to make the most of it.

Wind is the name we give to a moving airmass. The airmass can be quite small or it can be very large. However, whatever it's size, it has mass and is therefore affected by gravity, making it naturally sink towards the surface. It also has inertia, and once moving one way tends to carry on until something stops it.

When the sun warms the Earth's surface, this heat is transferred to the air lying on the surface; the molecules become more active in their movements, bounce off each other more strongly and therefore take up a greater space. This expanding air becomes lighter, the pressure becomes lower, it can hold more water vapour and it will tend to rise. Any cooler, heavier air lying on water or in shade, for example, will now flow into the low-pressure area and will be felt as wind.

Differential heating between different parts of the Earth's surface causes this basic pattern, which may be on a small scale as localised thermals, on a larger scale as a sea breeze developing on a coastline, or on a global scale, with trade winds blowing between permanent weather cells. Just to make this more interesting, half the world is in darkness and therefore cooling down at any one time, and the whole globe is spinning at 650mph. The result is that weather patterns can be quite complex, and the wind, rather than moving in a straight line, will tend to travel in a curve. For our purposes we need to know a little about the weather systems that affect our riding conditions, and a good grasp of the features of a synoptic chart (pressure map) as used on the more detailed TV or fax forecasts is invaluable.

This topic is covered in more detail in Chapter 7 'Weather assessment' . Our more pressing concern, however, is once on the beach, is the wind OK?

Wind Direction

Unless you are very expert, have a rescue boat following you, or are sailing in an enclosed area of water like a lake, the wind must be side-shore (blowing parallel to the beach) to some degree. For beginners, who are likely to progress downwind on each beat, a perfect side-shore or side-on-shore is best. Once you are confident of returning to your start point then some off-shore component become acceptable. A directly on-shore wind is difficult to use (if there is just one start point) as you will keep finding yourself back on the beach. An offshore wind is extremely dangerous as you have the opposite problem - you will keep finding yourself travelling out to sea. *Fig 5.1* shows the terms used for different wind directions.

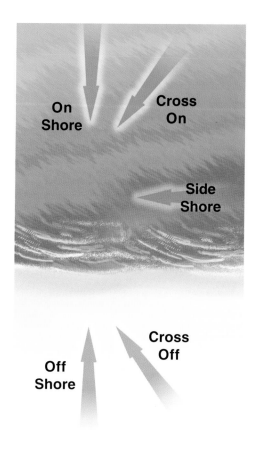

Fig 5.1: Wind Direction

Wind Strength

If the wind is too light then you will not generate adequate power to build up speed. A kiteboard needs to moving quickly to provide enough buoyancy to support your entire weight out of the water. Like a modern windsurfer it is designed for speed, and like an aircraft it will not work if it not moving! You will simply flounder and fall off. If you have access to a range of equipment, a larger kite or longer lines may just make the difference. If the wind is strong, power will not be a problem, but maintaining

control might be. If you cannot stand still on the ground with the kite stationary in the centre of the window, then you are likely to be overpowered and suffer problems controlling your direction. (And possibly your altitude!) Obviously, a rider with more experience, can control the kite in stronger winds than a novice, and different designs of kite and board also have a bearing on the useable range of conditions.

Wind Consistency

The third variable is the consistency of the wind. Those breezes flowing over large bodies of water like the sea are often quite smooth, but when they have been flowing over land, particularly if the terrain is high like mountains or cliffs, the flow can be turbulent.

Wind behaves almost like a liquid in its flow patterns, pouring down over cliffs and "rotoring" behind obstacles.(*Figs 5.2 & 5.3*) Inland bodies of water like lakes or estuaries, especially those surrounded by hills, trees or buildings can suffer from "bad" air making kitesurfing more difficult. Even at sea, if you are riding close to a headland or island, for example, or even a vessel that is upwind of you, you can expect the wind to curl around it and become unstable, with dead patches and gusts as you get closer to the obstacle.

It could be a bit embarrassing to be scudding past a ferry-load of admiring tourists when you suddenly slow down and sink... try and visualise the airflow towards you so that you are ready to avoid or make the most of any changes.

Unstable air with convection currents (thermals) can also cause gusty winds and a thermic flow is also often characterised by sudden changes in direction as well. Apart from the character of the wind, convection is often marked by cumulus clouds in the sky, circling birds, and darker patches of water where the thermal gusts ruffle the surface.

Approaching weather fronts and squalls can also change the strength and character of the wind in just a few minutes. As a rule of thumb, if the wind speed is varying by 100% or more in less than 3 minutes, the air is going to be very turbulent, and it may prove very hard to keep good kite control.

Wind assessment is important when you are choosing your launch point. A cross-shore wind may well mean that parts of the beach are in turbulent air, or windshadow from a nearby hillside or headland. It is not unusual to see families out for a day on the beach trying to launch their kites in a spot without a clean airflow and getting frustrated as they keep diving into the ground. *Figs 5.2 & 5.3* show typical wind flow patterns in a

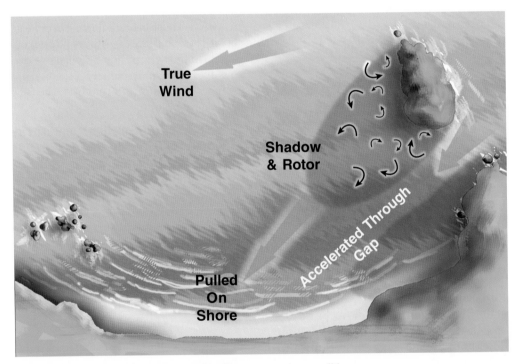

Fig 5.2: Windflow patterns in a small bay

Fig 5.3: Airflow over the landscape.

small bay.

The difference between a safe and enjoyable kitesurfing session and a nightmare of struggling for control can easily be down to your assessment of the conditions, so it is vital to check the forecasts, be careful and quit if it feels too much for you.

Photo: Cabrinha

Weather Assessment

Forecasts

Like almost all outdoor activities, we first need to decide what the weather is going to be like so that we can choose our venue or choose to stay at home.

Step one is to look out of the window, but the problem here is that you can only see what it is like now. What you need to know is how the weather will develop during the next few hours, and for that you need a forecast.

TV is very good on general weather; if it will be sunny or windy for example. From this you can gain a good idea of whether conditions are worth checking further. The better TV forecasts feature a synoptic chart with isobars (lines joining points of equal pressure) and frontal systems (*Fig 6.1*).

This type of chart is also available from the met office as a fax, or on the internet.

The simple rule when checking out a synoptic chart is that the closer together the isobars the stronger the wind will be. The wind strength and direction will be shown at various points on a chart but, inevitably not just where you want! To know the direction at a given spot, you

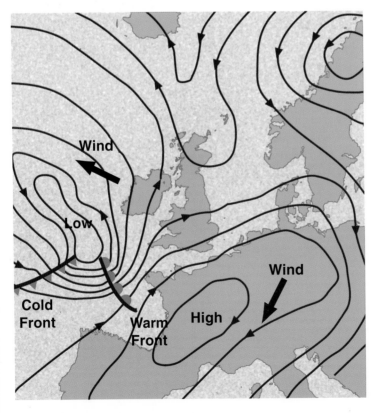

Fig 6.1: Synoptic chart showing isobars and frontal systems.

do need to be able to "read" the chart yourself.

The features of a chart are covered in the Meteorology section.

Useful forecasts can also be gained from the radio The best of these in the UK is undoubtedly the radio 4 shipping forecast. (Broadcast daily at 17.50) This gives actual readings from coastal stations and sea areas.

There are also a number of telephone forecasts that are available; these vary considerably between "it will be a nice day" to good accurate wind and weather data. In the UK they all get their information from the met office and you can get a list of what forecasts are available.

Some sailing and other sports clubs now have their own automated weather stations that you can access by 'phone. These give you the exact conditions and the trend over the last hour or two. The "Wendy Windblows " coastal stations are especially useful, as they are located at favourite windsurfing and kitesurfing spots and they also give tide states.

Details of these and other forecast sources can be found in Chapter 28, 'Useful Contacts'.

Tides

Another useful piece of information you may need if sailing on the coast is the state of the tide.

Tide tables can usually be purchased locally from a chandlers, or harbour masters office, on the internet, or checked by phone with your local kitesurf club or shop. You can even buy watches (Made by GUL) that can be set up to include a

A falling tide can expose hazards that were not a problem a few hours earlier.
(Photo: f8 Photography)

readout of the local tide state!

A kitesurfer moves fast and has only a small wetted area affected by the motion of the water. But the tide is still an important consideration to all riders, as a falling tide means hazards like submerged rocks can go from being unimportant to dangerous in the space of half an hour. Tides are not only the water level rising and falling, but are also responsible for tidal streams, which can travel at speeds of several knots along the coastline. If you find yourself paddling should the wind drop or your kit gets damaged, this may mean you cannot swim back to your start point. In certain areas, such as estuaries, the tide state can create strong onshore or offshore drifts. This can make the difference between safe enjoyable sailing and gradually being pushed offshore. It can certainly mean the difference between a short stroll and a long muddy paddle back to your clothes!

Basic meteorology

The weather is a huge and complex subject, but a grasp of the basic mechanics of a weather system will help you plan your venue more accurately and give you a good idea of what to expect next. Here is a quick guide to the main features.

Depressions & Fronts

Depressions are areas of relatively low atmospheric pressure. Air can rise easily in these regions and, as a result depressions are frequently associated with cloud and rain. Depressions often form where air masses of different temperatures meet. The division between these air masses is known as a front. Because the air masses on either side of the front have different characteristics, these fronts become irregular and develop "waves" along their length. The actual process is largely triggered by the high altitude jetstream winds.

A wave on the front is the first sign of a depression being created. As the depression develops, the pressure drops, and the winds increase. The air masses are now arranged in sectors (*Fig 6.2*), and are typically divided by a warm front followed by a cold front. As the depression gradually fills and weakens over the course of a few days, the cold front gradually overtakes the warm front and the result is an occluded front. Occlusions can be just like having one front turning into the next, giving miserable conditions for many hours, but quite often they are fairly weak and are marked by nothing more than a thickening band of cloud for an hour or two, or a few spots of rain.

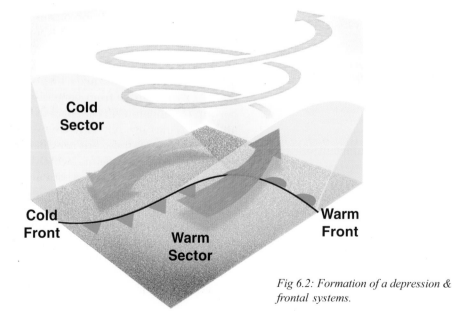

Cold Sector

Cold Front

Warm Sector

Warm Front

Fig 6.2: Formation of a depression & frontal systems.

Cold Sector

Warm Sector

High cirrus cloud thickens and lowers as front approaches Wind backs, rain.

Heavy rain on cold front, passes quickly.

Fig 6.3: Cross section through a cold front and a warm front

Wind will flow anti-clockwise around a low-pressure area. If you look at the synoptic chart in *fig 6.1* you will see that the wind direction is actually biased slightly inward toward the centre of the Low; rather like water flowing down a plug hole. (These directions are only true for the Northern Hemisphere. In the Southern Hemisphere the flow is in the opposite direction).

The majority of the "weather" is concentrated around the frontal zones, and to clarify the characteristics *fig 6.3* shows a cross section through each type of front.

A warm front is a simply the approaching warm light air sliding up over the denser cool air. It will first appear as high cirrus cloud a few hours before the front itself. This cloud gradually lowers and thickens into nimbo-stratus or strato-cumulus; these are rain clouds, and light rain will fall, growing heavier as the cloudbase drops. The wind "backs", that is it swings anti-clockwise, and strengthens. As the front passes over, the rain slackens, the cloudbase rises again and the wind "veers" (swings clockwise, from south to west for example). Though you

may not notice, you will now be in a warm sector with higher air temperatures. The passage of a warm front from the first sight of high cloud can take many hours, so once the rain starts you can expect it to last a while.

A cold front is similar, in that it "shovels" warm moist air upward ahead of it, but looks quite different to the ground observer. The first signs are heavy rain, and possibly thunder, with cumulo-nimbus clouds on an active front. There may be a "gust front" if the clouds are very large This is an area of strong wind, which may extend some way in front of the clouds, this type of sudden wind can be very dangerous. As the front arrives, the wind increases and veers. After the passage of a cold front, the cloud lifts quickly and the colder air may give a noticeable drop in temperature. Often, if the air is cold and the sun is shining, this may lead to thermal activity soon afterwards, with gusty winds. Cold fronts can be more violent than warm fronts because they travel faster and the warm air is pushed up more quickly. The whole front may arrive and be gone in a couple of hours, so if it is chucking it down when you arrive it may well be worth waiting.

High pressure systems

High pressure regions, or anti-cyclones, can be visualised as huge mounds of air. The additional weight of this air, which is constantly sinking and flowing downwards and outwards, acts as a lid that prevents thermals climbing to form cumulus clouds.

The weather in the summer is often hot and may be humid with little wind. When a strong high is established overhead, it may last many days, and unless a sea breeze occurs (*fig 6.4*), the kitesurfing possibilities will be very limited, as the winds will be very light.

In winter, the trapped warmer, more humid air can be cooled at night by contact with the cold ground, and fog or mist is common on high pressure days.

Micrometeorology

Once we have the basic picture from the forecast, we must add some local detail;

this is best predicted by being aware of the characteristics of the wind. It will tend to split around a headland, for example, but will be "pulled in" to a bay with high ground around it.

When the wind is cross-shore on any coast that is not straight, there will be areas of wind shadow behind promontories or any large obstacles such as rocks.

In places where the wind crosses land before a stretch of water then the airflow will be affected by the factors affecting that land, (e.g. thermals). A thermal is a bubble of air that is heated by a warm surface such as a town or a south facing slope. As the warm air expands and rises, nearby air rushes in to replace it, and the result is first felt by the rider as a lull and then as a gust of wind. Piled-up white cumulus clouds often mark thermals. The bigger and taller the clouds, the stronger the thermals. When conditions are good for this kind of convection, the air is referred to by weathermen as unstable,- and that is just how it feels.

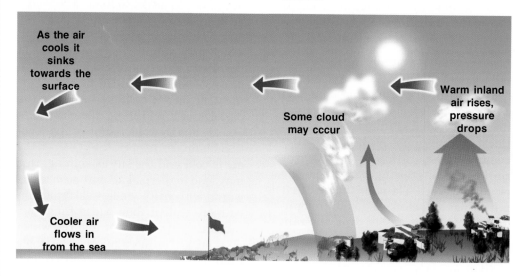

As the air cools it sinks towards the surface

Some cloud may cccur

Warm inland air rises, pressure drops

Cooler air flows in from the sea

Fig 6.4: Formation of a sea breeze.

Because air is affected by drag, and land is much rougher and therefore "draggier" than the sea, the wind a few hundred metres offshore is very often stronger than close in; so if the wind is close to your limit on the beach, be cautious how far out you venture.

Sea breezes

These are an important feature of coastal weather. A sea breeze is formed when there is a light prevailing wind or none at all, and the general heating of the land creates a lot of convection as the warm air rises. The cooler air lying on the water then flows in to the low pressure area inland and the breeze gradually swings more onshore and strengthens as the day progresses (*fig 6.4*). In the evening as the land cools more quickly than the sea, this process is reversed, so that at dusk the sea breeze may die away quickly and, as night falls, a land breeze may develop.

In many countries with warm climates this is a daily phenomenon, and the sea breezes around the UK coast are often force 3 and above on hot summer days, making apparently windless days quite usable to those in the right place.

Wind gradient

On the most detailed level, the main characteristic of the wind is the fact that it gets stronger the further it is from the surface (*fig 6.5*). This is simply due to the drag of the air on the water surface. In practice it means a kite at very low level will generate less power than one a few metres up.

Using longer lines and keeping the kite higher above the surface will often add power and make control more precise.

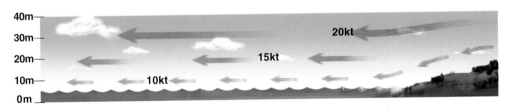

Fig 6.5: Wind gradient; the higher airflow is less affected by drag and is consequently travelling more quickly.

Setting Up & Launching the Kite

Before you even think of launching your kite, you need to check that there are no obstacles immediately downwind and that there are no overhead cables or power lines in the vicinity. You need to check the wind strength and direction to make sure you are in the right spot and are choosing the right kite.

It is very important that you ensure that there are no people or animals within range of your kite lines. When you have made sure the launch area is appropriate and safe, you are ready to set up your gear for launch.

Lay out your kite on its back, with the trailing edge facing the wind. If it is breezy you may need to put some sand or other weight on the kite to hold it still. Check that the bridle lines (those attached permanently to the kite) are tangle free.

Inflatable Kites

Inflatable kites must of course be pumped up; the best way to do this is to start with the ribs and leave the leading edge spar until last. This is not critical, but on many kites the valves are tucked in close to the main spar which, when inflated, may make access difficult, especially if they need to be pinched closed with one hand while the caps are inserted with the other.

Many of the inflatable kites have very ineffective one-way valves; you need to perfect the art of nipping them closed as you whip out the pump nozzle. The main spars are deliberately valve free so that they can be let down quickly in the wa-ter if necessary. Small hand pumps are easier to handle than large two-handed pumps and a useful tip with larger kites is to use the big pump to fill most of the chambers and the smaller pump for finishing the job neatly. If you only have a small hand pump, the big double handed versions can be bought cheaply from most toy shops where they sell kids' paddling pools.

It is convenient to drop the hand-pumps as you pinch the valve closed, but if it gets sandy it can easily score the bearing surfaces of the pump and in time will cease to work correctly. Setting up on a grassy area is the best bet if there is one available.

Using a hand pump. (Photo: R. Cruickshank)

When pumping up inflatable kites it is important to get as much pressure as you can into the spars. Whilst a soft kite will fly ok, it will buckle much more easily in a swell and will be much harder to re-launch.

Peter Lynn Arc showing valved cell entries and (inset) open rear deflation valve.

Large volume pumps are better for bigger jobs. (Photo: f8 Photography)

Ram-air Kites

Quite a few closed cell ram-air kites have very effective valved leading edges, and as a result it can be hard to get them inflated (if they are easy to fill with air then they are almost certain to get water in them if you drop them!). In order to get these kites inflated you need to either hold them up by the bridles and "pump" them a little to help the wind get in, or in lighter winds and especially with the larger kites, it is often quicker to start the process by using a big pump, just like the inflatable spar types. Once part full, these kites can usually be launched and will take a few minutes of flying to reach full efficiency. One note of caution

here: most closed cell types have a velcro dump valve on the tips or trailing edge to help you deflate them. Do not forget to make sure this is fully sealed before you start trying to fly the kite!

Once the kite is sorted you will need to attach the lines. All kite lines have colour-coded sleeves at each end so that you can ensure you have the right one. Decide which line goes where and then stick with that system. The normal nautical convention is that green goes on the right and red on the left, but of course you are looking backwards at the underneath of the kite so that means er....., well, its not important right now, as long as you remember what your system is! Many kites have colour-coded connection points which helps prevent confusion. You may have anything from two to five lines to connect and each connection should be made with a larks' head knot.

This knot looks very basic for something that is so vital, but provided it is tugged tight, the larks head has proved a virtually foolproof system. The harder they are pulled the more secure they become. Never connect a line with a regular knot; it shortens and weakens the line and after an hour under tension and wet it may be next to impossible to undo.

Knots must be made with the sleeved end provided; unsleeved dyneema line has an unfortunate tendency to cut through itself under shock loads.

Lark's Head knot. (Photo: R. Cruickshank)

Once everything is connected you need to move the kite into a position ready for launch. Whatever launch technique you choose, make sure the kite is secure, or someone is holding it for you before you start to walk away from it. The safest position is with one tip folded over and anchored down with a few handfuls of sand.

If you have a back-pack you can stuff your pump and bag into it to take with you, or stash it somewhere safe before you launch the kite. (*I advise against burying it and marking the spot with a sand castle!*)

A few handfuls of sand on the upper surface of the tip holds it down securely.

The lines will probably be wound around a bar; walk away from the kite into the wind, unwinding the lines as you go. You may find that if you unwind in one direction you will feed twists into the lines. Try a couple of loops, and if this is happening try swapping hands and unwinding the other way; this will usually solve this. Having the lines wound in a figure 8 pattern onto your bar is much better for avoiding tangles than simple loops.

Be careful not to tug the lines too hard as the kite may escape and take off before you are ready.

Once down near the bar end of the lines, check once more that you have no twists or tangles. If you have, then the best way to fix them is to put the bar down, walk back to your kite and "comb" the lines through your fingers as you return to the bar, This is much easier if you can get a friend to keep some tension on the lines.

Once sorted you are ready to buckle up your harness, attach your safety leash, move the admiring crowds back to a safe distance and launch the kite.

When on land, the kite can be launched either alone or with a helper. In either

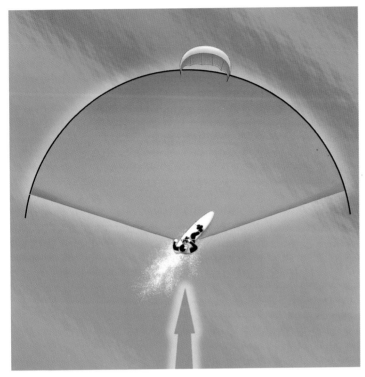

Fig 7.1: Plan view of the "window" of available kite positions the red band indicates the region of maximum power.

case, unless the wind is light, the launch is best done with the kite at or near the edge of the window. This is because the edge of the window (*Fig 7.1*) will allow you to launch without fully powering the kite.

In this way you can gauge the wind strength before you fly the kite through the middle of the "power band". It will make it easier to control and allow you to enter the water and sort out your board with fewer struggles.

If a friend is helping you, make sure that you brief them not to touch the lines, and to stand on the outside edge of the window or downwind from the kite. This will prevent them getting burned by fast moving lines should the kite launch unexpectedly; another reason to use the edge of the window.

There have already been cases of injury when a kite has been launched dead downwind on a breezy day. The sudden surge of power can pull you over and drag you, or in extreme cases lift you off the ground and carry you downwind for a nasty impact.

Launching Inflatables

Having put your kite in the optimum launch position near the edge of the window with one tip pointing into the wind, you may need to secure it if you are alone, while you return to the control bar or handles. A few kites will sit on the ground or can be parked "nose down" so that they do not move, but many will need securing, and a good handful of sand or small pebbles on a folded- over wing-tip will often do the trick.

Do not use heavy objects like rocks, especially if there are spectators around, as the launch can fling these quite a distance and you could damage your kite dragging the fabric out from under them. Given a suitable wind direction and strength, placing the kite into the water may add sufficient drag to hold it steady while you prepare.

As you walk back to your control bar, walk close to the line from the lower (into wind) tip. If it starts to move, a smartly placed boot will pin the line and prevent you losing the kite. Do not be tempted to grab fast moving lines with bare hands as they can give a nasty burn.

Some systems exist to allow you to launch the kite on very short lines and then "pay out" the line to the required length. In this case you may be able to self-launch simply by holding up the kite while hooked into it, and simply wind out the appropriate length of line required. This could be extremely handy on very small or restricted launch areas.

If your kite is fitted with a de-power system (i.e. has 3 or 4 lines) then it is not usually advisable to have the de-power system activated during the launch phase until you are very familiar with your kite's potential power in a range of winds. Only hook in when the kite is up and you are sure you are in control.

When you are holding the bar and have your safety leash connected, you can commence the launch. If you are self launching with a kite secured by sand it is simply a case of pulling the downwind (high) tip of the kite up into the airflow and the kite will move to the edge of the window and take off as soon as it starts generating lift.

If you have help, your launch assistant should stand downwind of the kite holding the leading edge vertically and pointing at the edge of the window so that it flies out of their hands. It is not necessary to throw it up into the air; launching towards the middle of the window or getting snagged by a line can be quite a problem, so any launch assistant should be well briefed before undertaking this task.

Launching Ram-air foils

Kites with closed cells for water use need to be inflated before they will operate properly (see above). To do this you can either allow the wind to enter the kite by holding it by the bridling over your head until it is half full, or (in light winds) stuffing the end of a pump into the cells

Ensure your launch assistant is well-briefed.
(Photo: f8 photography)

and manually pumping the first 30% of so of air into it.

Having done this you can lay the kite on its back and put some sand on the trailing edge before walking back to your bar or handles to commence the launch.

These kites may need to be flown for a few minutes before the internal pressure is sufficiently high for them to work properly.

Passers-by who try and help by grabbing the kite are more likely to cause problems than to help, so ask them (politely) to give you some space.

Obviously you must check that no peo-ple or animals are wandering over your lines when launching. If you stick to the edge of the window, and move the kite up the edge towards the zenith, the launch will be slow. If you start a low turn towards the centre of the window, the kite will accelerate and generate power very quickly. However, the act of turning loses power, and if you initiate a turn too early, when the kite is only just flying, it will tend to stall and dive to regain airspeed and may impact the ground and blow the launch. You can launch and fly a kite much more effectively if you understand how it works, which brings us onto basic aerodynamics.

Inflatables should be 'parked' by laying them on their bellies and anchoring them with sand or a board.

How the Kite Flies

There are a number of different kite de-signs available , but the basic principles of how they fly remain the same.

Drag

The simplest kite design simply catches the wind and pulls, just like a round para-chute or a paper bag blowing down the street. Very simply, the wind pushes on one side and creates high pressure. If you have a line attached, the pressure try-ing to push the kite along with the wind, pulls on the line. The larger the kite, the larger the dragging force.

Lift

If the kite is carefully shaped, the air-flow around it becomes more coherent and forms a primitive airfoil. All kitesurfing kites are of this type. The air flows in a curve over the top surface, and in doing so speeds up and creates lower pressure above the surface as well as higher pressure below. As the kite moves through the air, the airfoil acts as a wing, and generates lift as the pressure differ-ence tries to equalise (*fig 8.2*). Unlike a conventional sail that is static and relies on wind alone to generate this lift, a kite can fly back and forth at a good speed

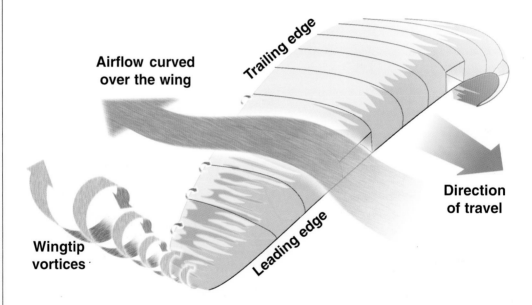

Airflow curved over the wing

Trailing edge

Direction of travel

Wingtip vortices

Leading edge

Fig 8.1: As the kite flies forward the airflow is split, with some flowing over the curved top surface and some flowing underneath. The upper airstream is accelerated over the curved wing and the pressure drops. At the tips this pressure difference is lost, as the air escapes around the edge of the wing and creates a rotating vortex or wake.

and is therefore able to generate a good deal of extra power.

The airfoil principle relies on the angle of attack being within the right range to work effectively. If the angle is too low then a soft airfoil (like those used in ram-air kites), will deform as internal pressure is lost, and even inflatable kites will drop the nose and enter a dive with the sail "luffed" (fluttering). This can be seen if the kite "overflies" the operator and collapses.

Turbulent air can also cause a momentary collapse or "tuck", though these usually only last a second or so until normal service is resumed.

The other extreme - a high angle of attack - means that the air can no longer travel in a smooth laminar flow over the top surface of the airfoil (*fig 8.23*). Imagine a smooth slab of rock in a stream. It can tilt so far with a smooth flow, but at

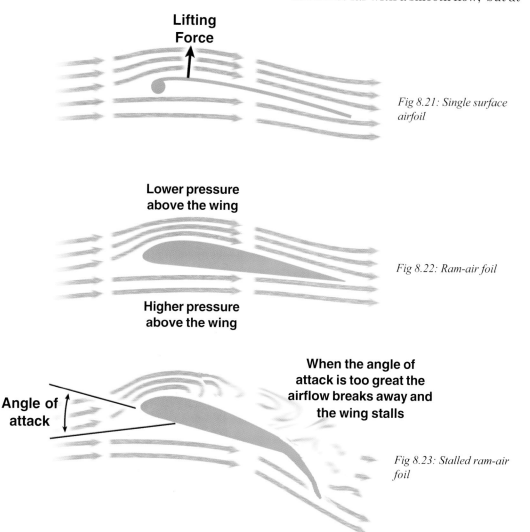

Lifting Force

Fig 8.21: Single surface airfoil

Lower pressure above the wing

Fig 8.22: Ram-air foil

Higher pressure above the wing

Angle of attack

When the angle of attack is too great the airflow breaks away and the wing stalls

Fig 8.23: Stalled ram-air foil

some point the water will break away and create a chaotic mass of white water behind the slab.

The same happens with air; too high an angle (usually caused by over-braking on a 4 line kite) - and the airflow breaks away and the kite loses all power. If the situation is not rectified it will then simply fall to earth...

The manufacturers of kites set up the angle of attack to be in the correct range, so provided the operator does not overbrake the kite, or the air become too turbulent, the kite will generate a steady pull.

Fig 8.2 shows that the same principle works for a single surfaced kite and for a fully formed airfoil section. These kites are now operating as true wings -if you were to hang a weight under them and drop them they would glide, just like a hang-glider or a paraglider. The full section airfoil with a curved top surface and a flattened bottom surface is more efficient at producing lift than the single skin designs, in the same way that an aeroplane wing is more efficient than a windsurfing sail. However, using a section like this for kitesurfing does have some drawbacks. A fully rigid wing section would be harder to transport and perhaps be easy to break if it hit the water. A ram-air inflatable section as used by many kites is much more practical, but of course if air can flow in, then inevitably it is easier for water to get in as well.

Many designers are working on ways around these problems, and it is interesting to see how the manufacturers of kites are resolving the challenges of building user-friendly but efficient foils.

How the kite is controlled

Kites have two basic control systems. The first is applicable to two-line kites and is simply load shifting. Increase the load on one side by pulling down on one line and the kite will distort and turn that way. Interestingly, when you do this, one of the first things to happen is that the lift is shifted to the other wing, and this encourages the kite to turn the other way. This phenomenon (known as adverse yaw) is most noticeable on kites with greater spans. However, the amount of load applied is generally so great that the kite has no choice but to turn towards the loaded wing. Control is simple but quite crude, just left or right. You cannot increase or decrease the speed or power by changing the angle of attack, for example.

True 4-line kites (i.e. those with independently applied control lines) are a little more complex. These are almost always ram-air types. The suspension lines take much of the load-bearing function, but steering is by using the separate control lines connecting the trailing edge of the kite to the handles.

The load-bearing front lines can be used

2 line kite on basic control bar.
(Photo: F-One Kitesurfing)

to steer in the same way as a two-line kite. The rear control lines (often referred to as brake lines) allow the pilot to pull down a "flap" on one side of the trailing edge, increasing the drag sharply on that side. The kite will react very quickly by turning in that direction. The control on a 4-line kite is far more precise than on a 2-line wing and multiple loops or spins are quite possible, where a typical 2-line kite will take up the whole window to make one 360% turn.

If both brakes are applied at once the kite can be made to fly at a higher angle of attack and will generate more lift and power. It will also fly more slowly, and so a 4-line system allows a greater power range and a greater range of windspeeds to be used efficiently.

If one control is applied hard (especially when the kite is moving slowly), the increase in angle on that side can be enough to make the airflow over the wing break up and stall that half of the wing. In this situation the kite will lose most of its power and will start to spin.

This is a great trick for stunt kite flying, but is less fun if you are kitesurfing. The lines will twist up very quickly, and once wrapped up a few times the twists in the lines can make the controls ineffective. The kite may just keep spinning until it hits the water.

If both sides of the kite are stalled simultaneously, the kite will simply stop flying and will fall backwards until the brakes are released.

This is a very useful safety feature, as it means a 4-line kite can be de-powered and dumped safely at any time, without letting go of the control bar or handles. It is impossible to de-power a 2-line system in this way. To safely dump a 2-line system, you must have a safety leash and drop the whole bar completely, with the attendant hassles of starting all over

(left) The Author & friend, synchronised flying with 4 line traction kites.
(Photo: f8 Photography)
(above) Cranked bar system.
(Photo: R Cruickshank)

again.

It is worth pointing out that the term "4-line" is often applied in Kitesurfing to what are really 2-line kites with a de-power system. Although they often actually have 4 lines, the depower lines are acting together and so they are strictly speaking 3-line systems!

This is not the same as having control lines as described above, but rather is a modification of a 2-line kite that allows the angle of attack to be changed in flight by raising or lowering the leading edge of the kite. You therefore have the advantage of varying the power, and so can use the kite in a wider wind range, but no advantage with the steering, which is still done with the basic load shift system.

This can be a bit confusing, especially as manufacturers and dealers often refer to up-grading a kite to 4 lines when they really mean adding a de-power system.

A "true" 4-line kite which can be stalled, launched backwards and spun by the operator is always fitted with separate handles. This system is normal for kite buggying and quite popular for snow kiting, but much less common on the water, as lacking a bar it cannot be easily controlled with just one hand.

A kite with a de-power system, on the other hand, is easily identified as it is always used with a bar, and usually one pair of lines are joined together and run through or around the centre of the bar with a smaller loop to activate them with your harness. This system is very common on kites designed exclusively for water use.

Types of Water Kite

Rigid spar kites

At the time of writing, kites using rigid spars like hang-gliders are very common for stunt kite applications, as they are incredibly sensitive and precise to handle. However, they are more prone to damage, particularly by waves, and in the larger sizes that are required for traction kite applications, they need battens inserted into the sail, to minimise fluttering, much like a full-sized hang-

A Mac Neptune (ram air water kite) with brakes fully applied. With this system the kite can be stalled and safely landed tail-first anywhere.

A Peter Lynn C-Quad 8.5m; it has a carbon rod along its leading edge. (Photo: Wind Designs)

glider. This makes them heavier and more costly.

As competitions become better established, this type of kite with its very wide window, high speed, and potentially better upwind performance may become more popular. I personally believe that the potential for into-wind glides from jumps and tricks like spins will see this type of wing gathering popularity. But at the present stage of the sport they are more commonly seen on land than on water. A big problem is that the generally fairly flat shape means that they lie on the surface when downed, making re-launch very tricky.

At the time of writing (March 2002) only one model (the Peter Lynn C-Quad) uses this pattern. The C Quad can be fitted with detachable floats to help the re-launch to a limited degree.

Ram-air kites

These are generally derived from those other flying machines, paragliders. And like paragliding canopies they benefit from using their own airspeed to remain inflated in an airfoil section. They provide excellent performance combined with easy use and are usually in 3 or 4-line configurations. They are almost unbreakable in normal use.

These types are very efficient and are the clear favourites for dry land kiting sports, the down side is that the cell entries required to inflate the wing are also potential entries for water if they are dumped in the sea.

The designers of the latest kitesurfing-specific models have devised ingenious valved inflation and drainage systems to minimise this problem, and a fully inflated wing may resist water flowing in

Ozone Razor ram-air kite.
(Photo: Ozone Kites)

in many situations, hopefully long enough to re-launch it. But, once the water is in, it is usually staying in, and as a result these kites are best suited to those who are confident that they will not be ditching the kite too often. Needless to say a waterlogged kite a few hundred metres off-shore is likely to mean a long swim.

They do have the potential to be the best and most flexible type of kite for the experienced rider. However at the time of writing, it is the case that for most new riders the spectre of serious re-launch problems if they should get water in them makes them less attractive than low aspect ratio inflatables.

Inflatable kites

Inflatable kites are those which work by having a leading edge tube and some ribs supporting the sail that are manually pumped up before use. The single surface and the "step" in the airfoil caused by the tube make them relatively inefficient as wings, but they have one major advantage over the other types - the fact that they can be re-launched from the water in a range of wind conditions. The original curved shape and inflatable rib design were patented by the Legaignoux bothers (founders of Wipika) and they have sold licences to a number of manufacturers who have either produced near clones of the design or increasingly are modifying the basic idea to produce a family of products.

Another related design is the straighter leading edge boom and paired inflatable ribs that typify the "Manta" design. Bic, Kitech, Seasmik and other manufacturers (mostly French) have adopted this system, which does have a considerably wider wind range than the Legaignoux types.

Other manufacturers have made some interesting attempts to refine the aerodynamics of inflatable wings, either by altering the tube layout like the Flexifoil Nexus models, or by incorporating battens, or by hiding the tube inside the section of the kite. At the time of writing none of these have made a big impact on the market., but there is huge scope for improvement so it is just a matter of time…

A curved shape supported by inflated ribs means that the floating wing will always have some part of the fabric protruding into the wind. This will drift downwind

Ram air water kite with valves (above).
(Photo: Advance Kites)
High aspect ratio inflatables at a competition venue (right).
(Photo: f8 Photography)
Low aspect ratio inflatable (below).
(Photo: R Cruickshank)

to line stretch position, allowing the pilot to manoeuvre it into place for a re-launch. Easy to fly and with slow handling, these wings are ideal for the first-time buyer. But because of their lack of flexibility in terms of wind range, a keen kitesurfer will soon need to buy 2 or more sizes if they are going to rely on this type of kite alone to give good riding in a range of winds. These are usually sold in a two-line configuration with a bar. But this type of kite can generally be modified to accept a de-power system to give more flexibility and a wider wind range.

Inflatable kites are available in a number of models, and the trend has moved towards kites with higher aspect ratios (slimmer shapes) as they are faster and more efficient in the air. They go upwind better, and because they are aimed at existing riders they are often supplied complete with a 4-line de-power system. Because of this higher specification *(and higher price!)* they are viewed as "better" by many riders.

Whilst this is true in terms of performance, it is unfortunately not true in terms of ease of use. Some of the larger high aspect wings that a rider might expect to use on light days are actually very poor at re-launching compared to their more basic low aspect cousins.

This is such a problem for the heavier kites in lighter winds that some are almost un-launchable in the weak conditions that they are most likely to be used in. Fortunately the newer models are being supplied with "reverse launching" set ups that mimic the characteristics of quad-line kites. These are discussed further in the section on control systems.

The Window

The window is the term used to describe the sector in which the kite will fly and generate power (*fig 9.1*). A stationary pilot can only fly his kite in this fixed area, but when the rider is moving the window moves with him.

The kite's speed and power depend to a great extent on what position it is occupying within the window. There are a few factors that we need to consider to understand how this works.

The drag on the kite is created by the wind. This is most apparent dead downwind; the kite is offering the greatest area to the wind in this position and so has the greatest drag

Because of wind gradient (see page 27) the wind speed just above the surface is relatively low so the best power is higher up the window. However, in the higher part of the sector the angle is poor, tending to pull the pilot up, rather than along, so this force is harder to use to generate foot pressure through the board and thus speed. The optimum area for usable power is around $1/_3$ of the way up the window and close to the centre.

If you have longer lines, you can get the kite up into the stronger wind whilst maintaining your optimum angle, though this may make the kite's handling a bit sluggish.

However, a modern kite is more than just a drag producing system. It also generates lift as it moves through the air and this contributes a good proportion of it's power. This means that the window is much wider and higher than if it were just a parachute. The window extends up to almost 90 degrees, (directly over

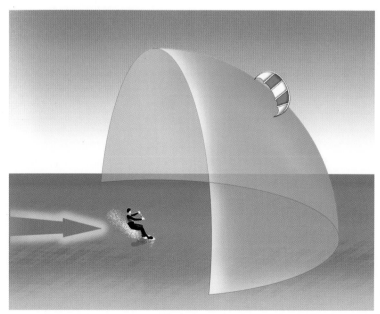

Fig 9.1: The 'Window'; the available sector of positions into which the kite can be flown.

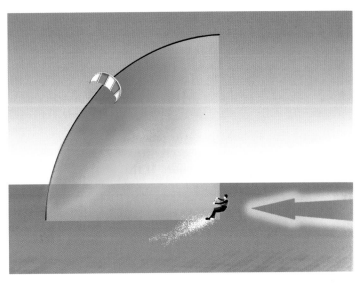

Fig 9.2: The window in section. The intensity of red shading equates to the amount of power generated.

the riders' head) - which is good for assisting jumps but not much good for generating any motive power. As a result this position is often referred to as the "secure" position as it is a safe place to park your kite. e.g. whilst you sort you board out. The width of the window is dependent upon the efficiency of the airfoil used, but inevitably as the kite comes close to heading into wind, and there is less tension in the lines, it will stop.

This means that the total window is effectively one quarter of a sphere, with you at the centre, a central sector that works efficiently - the "powerband"- and a peripheral region where the force becomes steadily less, the closer the kite flies to the edge.

The key to maximising power is to have the kite flying fast all the time to generate power from the lift, and keep it near the centre of the window to generate the most power from the push of the wind. This is not always possible, but the most effective way to keep the power strong

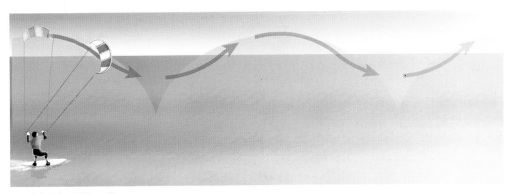

Fig 9.3: The "S" or Sine wave pattern.

and constant is to "work" the kite in a series of smooth S turns back and forth through the most powerful sector of the window. Because the flight path of the kite is like a horizontal letter S, this is often referred to as the "S" or sine wave pattern (*fig 9.3*).

Perfecting this skill is the key to smooth controllable power and, to a great extent, making kitesurfing easier. If the wind is strong enough you may find that the kite will provide sufficient traction power when just held still at the appropriate point. A few turns to get powered up and the board planing properly are very often required before you can relax and keep the kite in a set position.

In practice, you will find that in order to travel in the direction you wish, you will need to vary the position of the "S" turns within the window. This generally means being able to keep the smooth pattern mostly within the "front" half of the window. (i.e. in the direction of travel). If the kite is allowed to fly too wide into the rear half of the window, the board will either slow down, turn to follow, or if well powered up,- may jump out of the water entirely! If it flies too high up towards the secure position power will be lost. If it flies too far ahead to the edge of the window, the board will either try to follow, and stall as it turns upwind, or simply lose power until the kite is brought back into the powerband.

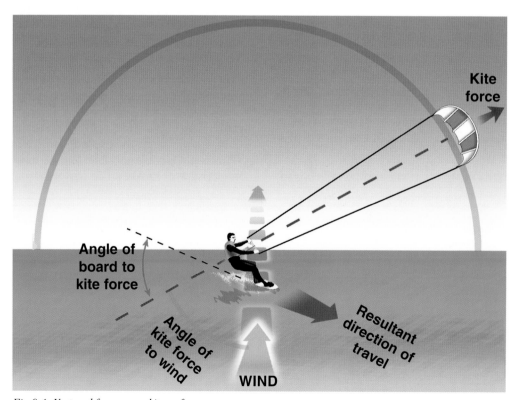

Fig 9.4: Vectored forces on a kitesurfer.

A good training programme should include plenty of practice at using the window effectively. If the kite can be worked smoothly in the correct sector, the power will be much easier to handle, and the rider will fall off their board a lot less often than one who is constantly changing direction and where the power is very "on-off" in nature.

The ability of the kite to fly at an angle to the direction of the wind is crucial as it allows the wind power to be vectored by as much as 30-40 degrees from the directly downwind course (*fig 9.4*). The shape of the board allows this power to be vectored by another 60-70 degrees, resulting in a course that is more than 90 degrees from the wind direction giving a slightly upwind direction of travel. This is illustrated in fig 9.4 and is explained in more detail in Chapter 20, 'The Points of Sailing'.

Kite Control Systems

Two-line kite with a bar

This is the most common configuration for beginners, and the easiest to handle. Turns are made by angling the bar and loading one line more than the other. A common problem is to try and steer the kite by turning the bar as if it were a cross-piece on a car steering wheel. If the lines remain under similar tension as you do this then of course nothing will happen! Some students like to use a movement that is both an angle and a twist combined (especially when body dragging) but it is important to note that only the increased tension on the shorter line is having any effect. The kite is best controlled by holding the bar close to the ends and keeping the arms as straight as possible. Having both hands high up in the air is extremely tiring as the blood needs to be pumped up to your arms, so the sooner a harness is introduced the better.

When the loop in the centre of the bar is hooked into the harness, not only does it relieve the arms but it also gives a handy pivot point. The kite can be well controlled with one hand by simply pushing or pulling one end of the bar. The closer together the line attachments on the bar the less effective the control inputs will be, so larger kites (or lighter winds) may dictate the lines being fixed further apart than smaller kites to give similar control authority. Some popular models of Kite have a choice of trim settings (more than one knot on the fore and aft connection lines), which allows you to set the angle of attack of the wing higher or lower. If the angle is set higher (i.e. rear lines shorter) the kite will generate a little more power.

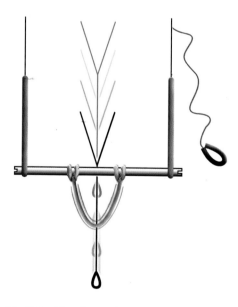

Fig 10.1: 2-line kite with bar configuration   *Fig 10.2: 4-line kite with bar & de-power system*

4-line depower system and bar

(*Fig 10.2*) This is the same as the 2-line system except that the de-power system is activated by hooking the harness hook into a smaller secondary loop in the centre of the bar (sometimes called a chicken loop). This loop is connected to the additional pair of lines. By applying pressure to the loop (allowing the bar to move away from your body) you can transfer the load to this pair of lines and so change the angle of attack of the airfoil (see Chapter 14). In this way the speed and power range of the kite can be broadened considerably.

(true) 4-line kite with a cranked bar

This system works by having the main load-bearing lines attached to a straight central section of the bar, and the brake or control lines attached to the ends of the bar, which are offset due to the angles in the tube (*fig 10.3*). If the bar is held in one plane and simply tilted like

a 2 line version, then the kite behaves in the same way and turns towards the shortened lines. However, the cranked bar has an additional capability in that it can be "twisted", allowing the main load-bearing lines to remain still whilst the brake lines are pulled shorter. This increases the angle of attack of the kite and adds considerable extra power. Because a 4-line kite has a much wider power range, it can be flown in a wider range of wind strengths, and at the upper limits is much safer to use as the kite can simply be stalled by applying enough brake to de-power the airfoil making it drop vertically to the surface. (Something that is impossible with a two-line kite, without resorting to dropping the bar and relying on a safety leash.) This is a good system in theory, but in fact it is difficult to operate effectively and it is now quite uncommon. It works most effectively with ram air kites. With prolonged use the twisting action can be a strain on the wrists.

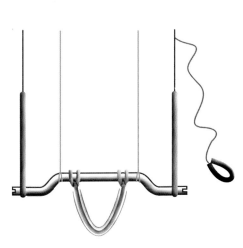

Fig 10.3: A 'true' 4-line kite with cranked bar.

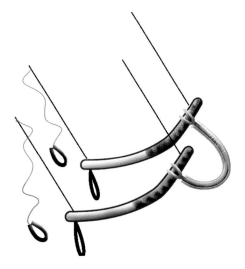

Fig 10.4: A 'true' 4-line kite with control handles.

(true) 4-line kite with control handles

(Fig 10.4) With this arrangement the wing can be flown very efficiently as the brakes can be applied one at a time, as conventional aerodynamic controls, making the kite far more manoeuvrable. (This is how paragliders are controlled). The kite can be turned very quickly, flown at a variety of angles of attack to control speed and lift, and can be accurately positioned in the window. The kite can also be induced to spin, useful for untwisting lines, but a nightmare if it happens accidentally and renders the controls useless.

Control handles require near-constant input, and it is much more difficult to free a hand for holding the board etc. It is also harder to feel what is happening to the kite if your eyes happen to be full of spray. If the handles are linked with a line to allow you to hook in your harness, they are pulled together, making gross movements a little awkward.

For all these reasons it is considered wisdom that 4-line control handle kites are only suited to experienced riders. The technical aspects make them less well suited to the new rider who is less likely to need the fine control and more likely to struggle with the difficulties of water starting with this system.

Control handles are the favoured system for buggies, snow kiting or other dry land users. This arrangement is only really effective on ram air kites or those with spars.

Pay out reels

Whilst not strictly a control system variation, the advent of "reels" fitted to the bar (designed to allow the lines to be lengthened and shortened for launching in restricted areas) offer the rider the option of changing the line length whilst riding. I cannot claim to have tried it, and do not know whether the current equipment is capable of being adjusted whilst under power, but certainly an over or under- powered rider can drop their kite and shorten or lengthen their lines before re-launching. Which could be a great advantage on some days. The company "Skyte" have pioneered these systems and market them for various kite models. If you are expecting to launch a kite from a very restricted area these accessories could be invaluable

Safety leashes

Any good kitesurf kite will be fitted with a safety leash. This is usually an additional line that is fixed a few metres up one load-bearing line of the kite with a Velcro wrist strap on the other end. If you drop the whole thing the load will be transmitted to the one line and the kite will flutter or spin down like a flag with virtually no power. Because you still have contact with the kite you can haul it back to you and (if you can sort out the mess) get ready to relaunch.

True 4-line kites that use quad handles are often not fitted with leashes on the understanding that the rider can always stall the kite by whacking on both brakes. Whilst this is usually possible when buggying, it is a dodgy assumption when snow kiting or wiping out in water, so a leash is recommended for these types as well.

True quad-line kites are best fitted with two short wrist leashes (kite killers) so that if the kite is dropped, the brake lines are applied equally and the kite will stall and fall trailing edge first without spinning. This makes recovery much easier than it would be from a spinning or nose-diving crash!

A safety leash being demonstrated.

Control Practice and Body Dragging

Once you have assessed the conditions and launched your kite, it is time to harness its power. Take a while on land to get used to using the window (a suggested training programme is outlined in Chapter 3). Get plenty of practice controlling the power by using the bar or controls and by stepping towards or backing away

The author gets in some control practice on the beach.
(Photo: R. Cruickshank)

from the kite. Have a go at spinning it and then recovering the twisted lines; the easiest method to do this is to hold the bar above your head and rotate your body under the kite. Get used to re-launching alone. If you can do this by dropping it into water while you are still on a beach or in shallow water, this will make it much easier to master the techniques of drifting the kite into the optimum launch position. The more practice you have with your kite on land the easier the transition to riding on a board will be. Many would-be kitesurfers are keen to dive in and ride before they have adequate kite control. Practice is the key to success, so take advantage of light or offshore winds to get some done!

Using your kite for buggying, snow kiting or particularly for powering a mountain board are all excellent practice, and can be done even when the conditions may be no good for kitesurfing.

Flying traction kites on land can be exhilarating but it can also be dangerous. Power assisted jumps can easily go wrong as you swing downwind under the kite, and injuries to ankles are easy to sustain.

If you should let go of your kite it can blow quite a way, and will not necessarily stop just because it touches down; it could endanger livestock, vehicles or people.

It is very important, therefore, that you have a wrist-leash to enable you to perform an emergency controlled descent. Using a large kitesurf kite on land can have much more painful consequences if it gets out of control than it would have on water; do be cautious in your assessment of the conditions.

Choose your flying area with care, and be especially aware of overhead power lines or other cables for obvious reasons. Always stop flying if dogs, livestock or people try to walk through your window (and they will!). A kite line can give a nasty burn and a 5-metre kite could lift a small terrier hanging on to it quite easily!

If the weather is thundery this can be a serious hazard, as the kite and lines may attract a lightning strike, especially if they are wet. There is a legal limit to how high you can fly a kite in the UK (60 metres); this is to prevent a hazard to low-flying aircraft. Needless to say, the approaches to airports or airbases are not suitable venues!

Once you are happy with your launches, control and landings, it is time to get into the water, but before you use a board for the first time it is best to practise using the kite in the water. In this way you can get used to the control differences and adapt to the "moving" window, You can have a lot of fun body-dragging through the surf even if you have not packed your

board! When body-dragging, useful exercises include working the kite back and forth through the power band of the window to produce maximum speed, using your body as a kind of "dagger board" like the keel of a boat, to travel as close to cross-wind as you can.

If you ever suffer a drop in the wind when out, or should lose or damage your board, you will need this skill to be able to recover yourself and your kite. Body-dragging is also an excellent exercise for practising kite control whilst looking where you are going rather than up at the kite itself.

The biggest single problem kitesurfers face is re-launching the kite when it is ditched in the water. It is worth spending a good deal of time learning how to get the downed kite where you want it and back into the air. This is easiest in shallow water without a board thrashing around, so do spend some time on these skills before trying to ride out into deep water.

If there is big surf which makes using the board impossible, you can have a lot of fun body-dragging, the only downside is that when you are laughing it is hard to prevent water getting in your mouth!

Controlled body-dragging.

Water Re-launching

The techniques for water-launching kites do vary from model to model, so ensure that you have read the manual so that you know what system works best for yours.

2/4 Line inflatable (low aspect ratio)

These are generally kites using the Legaignoux patent system. Manufacturers include Wipika, Naish, Cabrinha, Windtech, F-One, Flexifoil, Slingshot and others.

The commonst case is that the kite has ended up lying leading edge down with you looking at the undersurface. It is stable in this position and will not relaunch unless you turn it over.

Because of the heavy leading edge, inflatables often end up nose down!

If it is already in the "C" position simply start at stage 2!

1. Pull the bar strongly towards your chest then suddenly straighten your arms to slacken the lines. (If you can walk or swim toward the kite at this point that will help too) OR it occasionally works if you pull smoothly on one line then suddenly switch and pull hard on the other.

The kite (barely) in the C position. It is now tracking to edge of the window ready to be re-launched.

2. The Kite should flip over into the "C" position. By "playing" the tensions on the top and bottom lines you should be able to hold this position whilst the kite floats itself to the edge of the window. As it reaches the edge a smooth pull (more on the top tip lines than the bottom ones) may help it to clear the water and launch. Do not pull too early or it will turn over again and you may have to float it all the way to the other side of the window! The lighter the wind

the more delicate this operation!

If you have a 4-line de-power system, treat the right and left lines as pairs, but you may find that by holding some tension on your de-power loop the kite will drift faster and launch more quickly. (Especially heavier kites such as the LTR)

3. If the lines are twisted, most riders find it preferable to launch the kite first, then swivel the body to unwrap the lines once the kite is airborne.

4. Take the kite to the top of the window before attempting to re-start on your board. You may find it easier to loft the kite with the board floating nearby, then find your footstraps and water-start once the kite is up. However if the wind is light having your feet in the board and edging it hard as the kite drifts can help you hold more tension on the lines.

High aspect ratio inflatable kites

These tend to have longer heavier inflated booms and shorter ribs, and so they are generally more nose heavy, and can be very reluctant to flip onto their backs and get into the "C" position.

Subtlety does not cut much ice

in this situation!

If you gather in a couple of metres of the front (de-power) lines and wade/ swim toward the kite you should get a good bit of slack in the main lines; release the depower line(s) and the kite should turn over. From here you can get the wing

It's almost as much fun watching your mates struggling as it is doing it yourself!
(Photo: R. Cruickshank)

into the C position and drift it to the edge of the window.

Note: in very light winds with big (and therefore heavy) inflatable kites it can simply be impossible to re-launch them. So exercise caution about where you ride in this situation.

Ram-air kites on a bar with de-power systems

The pulling towards you trick is worse than useless with this type of kite, as pulling the cell entries through the water is virtually guaranteed to get water into the kite. The procedure for a nose-down kite is:

1. Hook into the bar loop with the harness.
2. Gather a couple of metres of the rearmost lines and pull hard. The kite should reverse upwards out of the water and you will feel a big surge of power.
3. If you are holding two separate lines, drop one line and the kite will spin round to the nose up-position. Drop the other a moment later, and if you have timed it right, the kite will fly up.

On some types you cannot hold the lines separately as they are connected closer to the kite. In this case drop the rear lines completely while steering hard one way with the bar, this should flick the inverted kite around and allow it to fly upwards.

This can be tricky to get right as you have to be both pretty brutal and spot on with your timing, but if done properly it is far quicker than dealing with most inflatable types.

Valved Ram air kites with control handles

If you have one of these you will already know how to reverse launch. This is a simple procedure: just apply both brakes to the nose-down kite, and as it flies up tail first, release one brake and it will spin into position and fly as normal. This is so quick and easy that it can be done by an expert almost before the board sinks. However if you do get water inside it is game over.

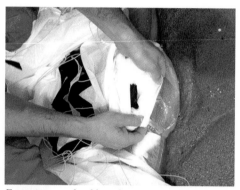

Emptying a valved kite that was immersed can be a major task. (Photo: R. Cruickshank)

Inflatable kites with re-launch systems

Some high aspect ratio inflatables now come with a re-launch set up to mimic the brakes of true 4-line kites. If you have one of these the procedure will be out-lined in the manual. Some may have an additional line specifically for this pur-pose.

This works perfectly on land or in strong winds but is not as easy when drifting.

*Relaunching a nose-down kite
backwards with a 5-line system.
(Photo: f8 Photography)*

How the Board Works

Kiteboards come in different shapes and sizes, each type having its own characteristics, as outlined below. However, the basic principles remain common to them all.

The board is generally smaller than all but the most radical windsurf boards, but in some respects it is designed to work in the same way. When moving fast over the water the board rides its own bow-wave in a process known as planing (*fig 13.1*). While a stationary or slow moving board will not support much weight and will sink when a rider stands on it, a planing board actually generates lift as it moves along, and the faster it goes the more weight it can support. In fact the lift a board produces is proportional to the angle of attack and the speed of the board squared. Or as I prefer to explain it: the faster the better.

The angle of attack is the angle of the lower surface of the board with the water. This varies with the amount of "rocker" or curve the designer has built

into your board, but is principally a function of your weight distribution. Too much power transmitted through the back or front foot and you can reduce the efficiency quite dramatically.

A common problem in lighter winds in particular is how to get the board onto the plane in the first place. A slow-moving board has a bow wave ahead of its centre of gravity (you) and the tail sinks as it is effectively trying to sail uphill. The key is to climb over this "hill" and start surfing down the other side. The summit of this wave is called the stagnation point, and a good burst of power is required for the board to climb over it. This may mean either pointing the board on a more downwind heading, or a strong and radical swoop of the kite, or a combination of both in order to achieve the plane.

Once the board is planing, the drag reduces significantly and therefore the power required to maintain it is noticeably less. The faster the board is travel-

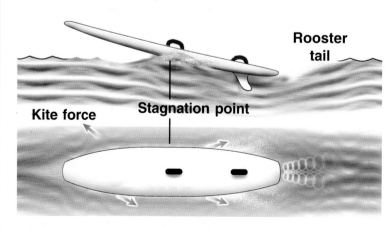

Rooster tail

Kite force   **Stagnation point**

Fig 13.1: A planing board, in elevation (top) and plan (below).

ling, the less area is in contact with the water and the lower the drag.

Windsurfers sometimes enquire about the volume of a board. In fact this is not relevant to kiteboards except in the lightest winds. Volume is a way of describing the flotation characteristics of a board - important if you are up-hauling a windsurf sail whilst standing on a board - but of no consequence when you are planing, and all kitesurfing is (hopefully) done on the plane. The size of board is really more concerned with the area that is in contact with the water and the manouvreability. Except in the very lightest winds rider height rather than weight is the critical factor . A tall rider needs a longer board, but a heavier rider does not, (he just needs a bigger kite).

When the board is on the move the tendency - especially in stronger winds - is for it to try and slide towards the kite. By pushing the inner (heel side) edge into the water the rider can tilt or "edge" the board and prevent it from following this course (*fig 13.2*).

It is a similar situation to bicycle on a hill, trying to roll to a point off to one side. Gravity is the motive force pulling it vertically downwards, but as the surface of the hill is in the way, the bike follows the easiest remaining course,

A directional board showing curved profile. (Photo: R. Cruickshank)

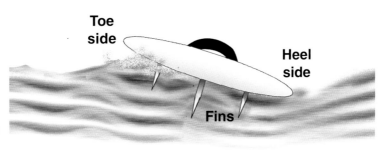

Fig 13.2: Rear view of an edged kiteboard.

which is to travel down the slope. To continue this analogy: if you edge the board too much, or try and point too far upwind of the kite, the power will not be adequate and the board will come off the plane and eventually stall, just like the bike trying to turn back up the hill. But if you go with the kite on a very downwind course you will get a fast ride, but probably not in the direction you want.

If you do not edge the board it will still try and hold a course, though less efficiently, as the fins provide some directional stability. The fins themselves act as foils and generate lift which act to prevent the board skidding sideways. This is good in one way and bad in another. Where there is lift there is drag, and the bigger the fins the more they slow you down. However, a board with a larger fin or number of fins will be more directionally stable, and will be easier to sail upwind. (Sailing dinghies and yachts can sail upwind very well, in part due to their relatively massive keels or daggerboards).

Kiteboards, however, generally use the whole edge of the board as a gripping device, so fins are generally kept quite small. They are simply there to prevent the board breaking away and spinning out as the lateral pressures build up. Many boards use 3, 5 or even more of these small fins.

A larger fin helps with directional control and provides a pivot point for the gybe, and so is more appropriate for a windsurf board. Fins are also

A small board needs to be edged hard to prevent it skidding away, especially when starting.
(Photo: f8 Photography)

a bit of a hazard when the board is surfing around in the waves next to you. A big fin can also cause control problems when the board is being deliberately pivoted in the "wrong" direction, when putting on the foot-straps during a water-start in strong conditions etc.

Large fins are also inappropriate on twin tip boards that do not need to be gybed.

You can kitesurf with an old windsurf board or with a surfboard (though both need the straps moving forward). It has been done with waterskis and even with a snowboard (although the snowboard did sink, which proved quite challenging). However, most riders will choose to use a purpose-built board.

These fall into three basic categories;

Directionals

These are the original design of kiteboard, and the rocker (curve of the undersurface) and asymmetric shape mean that they can only be ridden in one direction. To reverse your heading you probably need to perform a gybe turn and change your feet positions.

They are generally high volume and are pretty stable, making them ideal for lighter conditions and for learners, and the shape offers good upwind performance and great wave riding. Windsurfers will feel at home on one of these!

Wakeboards

Wakeboards often have a short waterline and either tiny fins or channels in the underside. Boards of this type are somewhat harder to sail upwind, and will "skid" more easily unless ridden at quite acutely tilted angles. The grippy shape and sharp rails mean that they can be controlled when conditions are very powerful.

Their lack of size makes them both manoeuvrable and good for jumping.

Most wakeboards have very little volume and are next to useless for supporting any weight. This means that they cannot be ridden in light wind conditions and are a problem if you do need to swim back to

Directional boards.

Wakeboard with full bindings. (Photo: Cabrinha)

shore.

They are great for high-wind blasting and jumping particularly when you have a friendly beach downwind (or a buddy with a jetski!)

Wakeboards are (usually) bi-directional and instead of using footstraps tend to use bindings. These can either be of the "sandal" variety, which can be pulled on with one hand and treated almost like footstraps, or true bindings which are very like ski boots and lock the rider to the board.

The Bic Airflow, a high-volume assymetric twin tip design. (Photo: f8 Photography)

This is very secure but means that starting is quite a bit more technical. Not only that, but they struggle badly if the wind is gusty.

For all these reasons they are not very suitable for the first time buyer unless you are already a wakeboarder. But if you want to get really big air, then eventually you may opt for one of these, as small boards are the best way to use big kites in strong winds.

Twin tips

Usually slightly larger than true wakeboards, TT's are generally fitted with foot straps like directionals, but with a symmetrical shape that allows you to choose whether to gybe or to just reverse course like a wakeboard. This seems like the perfect solution, and they are certainly very popular with the top riders, as they can do all the tricks with them. But like all compromises they are not quite as good at some things as more specialised boards.

Because you do not need to gybe, it is likely that twin tips will be the most popular class for many kitesurfers. (Especially if you can change the fin configuration for different conditions.) Some (like the Bic Airflow pictured left) are asymmetric, i.e. dedicated to being used for reversing course rather than gybing; they are shaped to allow use of just one rail. Others are basically double ended directional boards, and can be reversed or gybed.

Some larger twin-tips can be set up and ridden as adirectional simply by altering the footstrap and fin configuration. These boards (known as "mutants") do give the rider some additional flexibility, though they are are not a different type of board, simply a TT board with additional locating holes.

Advice on what type of board you should get initially really depends on the conditions you will be riding in. Directional boards with some volume and length are far better at dealing with a shorebreak that is commonly found on beaches with an onshore or side-shore wind, and they are also better at coping with the inconsistent power generated by inexperienced riders or simply poor conditions.

Twin tips are easier to turn without gybing, and are very well suited to strong conditions or flat water where the rider can edge the board strongly to avoid skidding without having to worry about finding themselves up to the knees in the next wave.

There have been large boards configured as Twin tips but they are not (in my view) ideal. Twin tips do need to be small, (or possibly have additional footstraps) as taking a symmetrical stance on a big board means that you will not have very good control authority, and where the nose of the board needs to be kept up in waves, you may end up riding with one leg doing all the work!

Leashes

All boards with foot-straps need to be attached to the rider with a leash. The leash prevents losing the board when you fall off and can also be helpful for handling the board as you get your feet into the straps. The leash should be around 2 metres long and preferably have a velcro or snap hook attachment that can be managed with one hand. Many riders fit the leash to their ankle, but snapping it to part of the harness is becoming increasingly popular as it is easier to hook in with one hand. (It may also help prevent tangles). Riding with a leash that is too short can mean the board keeps whacking you in the legs when you are not on it, and a long leash can be a huge hazard, as the board can get well away from you or easily surf back at some speed to hit you in the head or disappear between your kite lines.

Using a 3m leash in surf was partly responsible for one rider ending up with both legs tied together in coils of leash after being "rolled" when he had fallen off. (People who kitesurf generally love to look cool, but you also have to be prepared to look a total idiot! - sorry no picture!)

From Left to right: Windsurf board (for comparison); typical directional; surfboard with footstraps; twin tip with footstraps; small twin tip with sandal bindings. (The small board in the foreground is a skimboard. These are finless and are no good for deep water or going upwind but huge fun in 1cm of water with a power kite!)

Footstraps are important too; they must be positioned correctly, as a nose low or high position can make a massive difference to the boards efficiency. To start, it is better to have them positioned quite far forward. This helps you keep the board flat and prevents turning upwind. Once you are blasting you can always shift them back a bit. It is a pain to lose your board, but nevertheless they should be open enough for easy location with your booted foot. Again, you can always tighten them later if you need more security for big jumps.

Wakeboards will often use bindings for your feet, but these are not so good for boards with any volume, as you might find the board floating behind you, and it may be impossible to sink it by single-handed muscle power alone to get it back into position.

Sandal bindings, a coiled leash and footstraps are visible on the other board.

Footstraps with an ankle elastic (sandal bindings) have also been tried, but like true bindings they are generally not a good idea on boards of any size. Apart from anything else, if you do lose one, your remaining foot is locked in by the other, and the potential for nasty injuries to your leg joints as the board is wrenched around is a serious deterrent.

Boards are constructed from a variety of materials, ranging from PVC/foam sandwiches, fibreglass, epoxy resins, to carbon fibre, metal and even wood. The fact is that the manufacturer chooses the materials on a combination of stiffness, flexibility, and, of course, price. There is no "right" material. Any good dealer should be able to explain the pros and cons of each model.

Before you buy, you should carefully consider all these factors, and only then should you buy the one with the coolest graphics.

Bigger directionals may be harder to control during large jumps.
(Photo: F-One Kitesurfing)

Using the Board

At this point in your training programme you have mastered the kite, done some body-dragging and a few water re-launches and know quite a bit about the theory of boards. It is time to put it all together.

There are a number of different types of board as discussed in the previous chapter, but many new kitesurfers will be using a standard directional, i.e. a reasonably large volume board which has a nose and a tail with 3 footstraps. This section assumes that this is the type you are using.

Before using the board you first need to ensure that it is set up correctly. This is best done away from sand and water! The fins must be properly located and screwed in; they tend to be a tight fit and locating the locking plates or screw threads can be tricky. It is very important that fins are secure, as losing one will be a serious problem on the water.

Note here that fins can be quite fragile; remember this when handling the board,

Fitting fins. (Photo: R. Cruickshank)

especially if you are in shallow water or near rocks.

Any anti-slip deckpads must be fitted; these are usually self-adhesive, and again, any sand or water will prevent them sticking firmly. The footstraps must be set up so that you can easily push your feet in (probably whilst wearing neoprene bootees.) Footstrap positioning is important, but initially it is probably best to locate them reasonably well forward (many beginners tend to sink the tail of the board). When you are blasting regularly you can always shift them back a bit.

The leash must also be firmly attached before you venture into the water. There is usually a fitting point for this on the board.

When you are ready to use the board, the easiest option (if the area and conditions allow) is to launch the kite on land and manoeuvre it into a stable low power position at the top of the window. Assuming that you are using a board with footstraps, the board should be lying close by. With practice you should now be able to hook your harness into the control bar loop and keep control by pivoting the bar with one hand on the harness.

With your free hand, fasten the leash to your ankle or harness, scoop up your board and walk steadily into the water, keeping the kite in the stable position as you do so.

As soon as the water is deep enough to allow you to use the board without the fins grounding, you can sit back in the water, align the board the way you wish

Controlling the kite with one hand.
(Photo: Advance kites)

to travel (at say 120 degrees from the wind direction) and use your free hand to help your feet into the footstraps.

The easiest way to do this is to insert the front foot first, while holding the rear footstrap with your free hand. Then switch the hand to grip the leash at the back of the board and use that leverage to insert the back foot.

Unhook to give yourself the most scope for manoeuvre, check that the direction you are heading is clear, and you are ready to power up the kite! Just as in the land-based exercise, you will need to dive the kite into the power zone on the leading edge (front) side of the window.

You will get a quick shampoo and rinse if you wipe out; you will sink or fall back if the wind is not sufficient; or (hopefully) be pulled smoothly into the upright position and sail away!

Students turn next : A helping hand is a big advantage to start with.

Initially, you are bound to have a few problems. The board may skew to point up or down-wind while you are preparing. You can use the kite to help orientate it again, but if you should turn too far you will lose control, and have no option but to take your feet out and start again. The first few attempts are always much easier with a little help to steady you as you get used to the board. There is no substitute for an experienced helper at this stage.

Put your front foot in ...

put your back foot in ...

and sail away!

Don't lean back too far..

The more you have previously practiced with the kite the easier this will be.

Balance is principally concerned with keeping your knees slightly flexed to absorb the bumps, at the same time keeping you eyes mostly on the kite. (You do need to glance around as well, to ensure you are not converging on other water users). Because the pressure on the lines is less than when you are standing on land, the kite may seem more sluggish to respond, so work it strongly to keep the power smooth. Stance is important here; many riders stick their backsides out and use the "backache" position.

... or forward...

Once up on the board there is quite a bit to think about. Not only do you need to keep the kite moving in a smooth S pattern in the leading half of the window, you also need to keep the board steady in its direction and maintain your balance.

And he's up! The nose of the board is high, but the rider is about to dive the kite forward, which should help him move his weight onto the front foot and accelerate the board.

Once you can trust the power of the kite you can lean back and straighten your body to adopt a better stance. This is helped a great deal by hooking back into the loop on the bar with your harness.

A common fault while all this is going on is to allow the board to head up into wind. Once the board is pointing one way and the kite another, the next move is to get pulled off! Alternatively some riders, anxious to keep power on, gradually head down-wind until the kite is in front of the nose of the board. This also generally results in a quick swim! The board can only work effectively when the power is applied through your feet and the direction is somewhere between 20 degrees upwind and around 70 degrees downwind. For the first few attempts, a course of about 10-20 degrees downwind is the easiest to cope with.

Common start problems

Falling backwards is usually a result of not having enough power. A determined swoop of the kite and strong S turns will give good power. If this is still not effective, try a larger kite, longer lines, or aiming a little more downwind.

Falling forwards is a problem of balance and overpowering. Bend your knees more, fly the kite a little lower, and edge the board hard as you are pulled up. Try aiming a little further upwind. You may need a smaller kite, or to wait for conditions to weaken a bit. Some students find the board keeps pointing upwind. This is a result of putting almost all the pressure through your rear heel. To compensate you must use the front leg more and try to flatten the board with toe pressure.

The opposite problem is that the board keeps following the kite downwind. The solution is also the opposite - give it plenty of heel pressure to dig in the board's edge. The next danger point is when the kite is turned for the "upstroke" of the pattern and some power is lost. The key here is to have had plenty of practice at working the kite for smooth power and bending your knees to absorb the changes in pull... practice is the only way to improve!

Once you are travelling reasonably comfortably, you can relieve the pressure on your arms by hooking in with your harness. This does have the effect of reducing your turn input to some extent, and is often done when the kite is generating sufficient power to be effective without being "worked" as hard.

Wakeboards

If you are using a wakeboard or similar device with bindings, then you have no option but to launch the kite after you have done them up and are on board. This is a little trickier in some ways (especially in high winds,) and it could be a bit embarrassing wiping out on the beach with a wakeboard attached. A launch from shallow water is your best option until you are very confident of your gear.

Because a wakeboard is typically channeled, or has tiny fins rather than having thruster fins or skegs, it is sometimes possible to "skateboard" over wet sand like a skimboarder and slide straight into the water. Be aware however, that it may look cool, but it will eventually damage the underside of the board.

Wakeboards and small twin tips are usually favoured by riders who are quite experienced and who want to ride in stronger conditions. They are particu-

larly suitable for those who want to get some serious air!

Controlling the board

There are three major considerations - maintaining your direction, controlling your speed, and making turns.

Maintaining direction is often managed almost automatically by riders - particularly those with some windsurfing, or other boarding experience. The board reacts to foot pressure and the resulting changes in drag from the water. So, if you press down on the far side of the board with the toes of your feet, the drag on that side will increase, the board will flatten or tip that way, swing downwind and will start to gybe. If you press with your heels, the board will edge the heel-side rail and, if the rear foot is applying the most pressure, the nose will swing upwind. As you practice, steering will become second nature. The important factor is to keep looking where you are going. Two key mistakes are fixing your

Take one small board, add a big kite, warm sea, strong wind...& mix well! (Photo: F-One Kitesurfing)

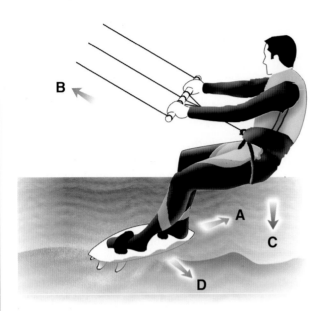

Fig 14.1: Forces on the board and rider. To hold a course, A, the forces must be balanced. A strong pull from the kite, B, must be countered by more weight (leaning back), C, and more drag (edging the board harder), D.

gaze on the kite and looking down at the board. It is rather like looking in the mirror in a car, or down at the gear lever; very useful at times, but too much and you soon lose your bearings and cannot hold a course.

Controlling speed is done in a couple of ways. You can reduce the traction power of the kite by pulling it up to the top of the window. This works well and is safe, but does mean you are likely to change course and travel further downwind. An alternative is to create more drag by edging the board harder. i.e. by pressing the rail harder into the water and leaning back. This, combined with moving the kite closer to the front edge of the window, allows you to hold your course, or

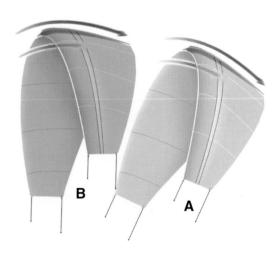

Fig 14.2: The illustration shows how the trimmed angle of attack of the kite (A) is lowered by the application of the de-power system (B) as the load is taken by the shortened lines attached at the front of the kite.

make better progress upwind.

If you need to add speed, this is best achieved by minimising the drag, i.e. keeping the board flat, working the kite fast and quite low in the window, and by choosing a slightly downwind direction if that is appropriate.

If you have a de-power system on your kite, the power can be well controlled by adding or removing pressure through your harness hook, and altering the angle of attack and thus the power of the kite. *(see fig 14.2)*The higher the angle of attack of the kite the more lift and power will be generated. This is a big advantage of kites of this kind, but does make their use a little more technical.

Most kites now being sold can be used with de-power systems (often confusingly referred to as 4-line kites). Typically (but not always), the two front lines are connected to a single point somewhere along their length, and this line is connected in turn to a smaller loop on a sliding system in the centre of your bar. The harness can be hooked into this loop (often called a chicken loop) to increase or decrease power. Such a system makes the kite a 2-line model from a steering point of view but a 4-line kite from a power variation point of view. This system, in conjunction with good board control,

gives a good range of options for managing the power of your kite.

Speed and direction are the critical elements to master, but dealing with waves is also important. A good rider will anticipate the water's movement and ensure that the nose of the board does not get buried in a swell by moving his weight back as he hits a wave. As you plane down the other side the weight can move forward again to maximize speed and prevent the board from stalling.

Shorter boards need good power management as they are generally less buoyant and are therefore less tolerant of lapses of power. If you are riding a smallish board in weaker conditions, the balance of maintaining power whilst edging for direction can be quite subtle. This is one of the reasons that as boards get smaller so kites are getting bigger!

Stance is critical on shorter boards, and twin tips will require a conscious effort to bias the load onto the rear foot in anything other than flat conditions.

Whatever equipment is employed, a rider will soon get used to making small steering and speed adjustments as a matter of instinct. The key is plenty of practice!

Making turns is covered in more detail in the next section, 'Changing Direction'.

Changing Direction

A rider can make adjustments to his heading by moving the kite in the window and by edging or steering the board through foot pressure, but this only allows small directional changes. As soon as you are doing good runs, you will need to reverse direction and ride back the way you have come. The method that you will probably use first is to step off the board, float it around to change foot position and re-start. This is effective, but not exactly cool, and it does involve a good deal of drifting down-wind. What you need is a quick turn so that you can at least get back to your start point, or preferably make upwind progress if required.

There are three distinct ways to do this:

1. Toe-down riding.

In normal riding your heels are down (i.e. edging the board on the side beneath your heels). In this position your body is only slightly twisted, as the kite is usually in front and to one side of you. However, it is quite possible to ride with the toe side down. In this position your body is twisted at least 90 degrees and the kite is to one side and slightly behind you. By switching from heel-down to toe-down position you can turn the board but do not need to swap your feet around in the straps.

- Loft the kite into the neutral position above you.
- Pivot the board down-wind and press down with your toes to carve a turn.
- Keep carving and let your body twist to follow the kite
- Bring the kite down into the new front

window position.

- You will need to continue to dig in your toes as you work the kite as it easy to relax and let the board turn downwind.

To turn back is easy; just take the kite back to the original front of the window and follow it around with the board.

Riding toe down feels strange at first, but it is great fun and the position of leaning forward towards the water gives you an even greater sense of speed than being the "right" way up.

Toe-down is so called as the board is edged with the toes instead of the heels.
(Photo: Advance Kites)

There are certain asymmetric board designs that make toe-down riding impractical.

2. Gybing. (Jibing in the US)

What is a gybe?

There are two recognised methods of turning a sailing craft: the tack and the gybe.In other forms of sailing craft the hull or board can be turned through the upwind zone to perform a tack.

Under normal circumstances a directional kiteboard can only reverse its direction by turning the nose of the board through the downwind zone and therefore performing a gybe.

This does have a disadvantage when you are trying to make upwind progress, as the rider will inevitably find that they move downwind during the gybe; but on the plus side gybing turns are fully-powered, making them fast and exciting, and allowing you (with practice!) to keep the board on the plane.

How to Gybe.

There are two variations of the basic technique - moving the feet before carving the turn and moving the feet afterwards. The second is perhaps a little trickier to master, but may be favoured by windsurfers as it is based on the classic windsurfing gybe.

In all cases, the best way to start is to ensure that you are riding smoothly and not too overpowered - if you are edging the board hard or leaning back then gybing will

be much harder. While it is not mandatory, to begin with it is advisable to unhook before you initiate the turn.

Feet first varation:

- Take your feet out of the straps and when you feel balanced switch your "old" rear foot to the new front strap (or more likely on top of it or next to it).

- Immediately move the old front foot back and place it next to the rear strap. (The kite should be moving across the top of the window at this point and the board will be turning downwind).

- Carve the board around by pressing on the downwind rail with the new back foot.

- As the board comes around onto the new heading you need to complete the dance by placing the "old" front foot into the rear strap.

Performing a gybe with a directional board.

- Bring the kite down into the new front half of the window
- Finish off by slipping the old rear foot into the front strap.

Feet last variation.

- Take the rear foot out of the straps, but keep it in that general area.
- Press with the toes of the rear foot to carve the board; keep your feet still until the board is round onto its new heading. You are now sailing in the "toe down" position".
- As soon as you feel balanced, switch your feet; then slip them into the foot-straps.

While you are moving your feet around, the kite should be lofted to the higher edge of the window, and, as the board is carved around, pulled down into the new leading quarter of the window. The lift created by the kite minimises your weight on the board and makes the whole thing more stable as you move your feet.

Even if the gybe is a bit slow at first, and de-powers the board, you should be in a position to immediately dive the kite and power up again as you complete the turn. Plenty of successful gybes involve a moment spent almost squatting in the water!

No words can explain the feel of the turn; each board will react differently depending on its volume and width. Like most things it is a question of practice, judging the right moment to move your feet, and keeping your knees bent and movements fluid.

Like most exercises requiring balance and co-ordination there is no substitute for watching a competent rider demonstrate a few times and then just keep practicing.

Note: because you will be moving your feet in and out of the straps they must be set with sufficient play to let you do this easily.

Unhook, loft the kite and start to carve the board round...
(Photo: F-One Kitesurfing)

3. Turning Twin-Tip boards.

The third method of turning is simply to make the front of the board into the back and ride tail first. In the early days this was a freestyle trick, but with the advent of twin-tip boards and symmetrical foot straps, it has become the easiest way of all to switch direction on a kiteboard. The advantages are obvious - no downwind turn means less loss of progress if you are beating upwind - and no necessity to move the feet means less chance of losing balance or missing a footstrap. All that is required is to shift the weight from the old back foot to the new back foot as the kite changes direction. The board can remain edged during this change and so there is almost no drift if executed swiftly.

Most twin-tips are quite small, so if the direction switch is slow they tend to wallow, or in strong winds you can find yourself inadvertently taking off if the kite is allowed to get too high. However, with a little practice it is a straightforward manoeuvre.

Some top riders like twin-tips because of the potential for different tricks, but many new riders choose them primarily for the simplicity of the turn control. And while this is of course not the only parameter for choosing a board, it is a big attraction of twin-tip boards.

The versatility of a twin-tip board.
(Photo: f8 Photography)

Dealing With Light & Strong Winds

By now you may have already discovered that the wind is never perfect (except on the days you have missed!). Apart from wind direction, it is almost always either too light or too strong (or sometimes both on the same day). However, the range of winds that you can use given the right techniques and equipment is surprising.

Light winds

If the wind is light when you arrive at the beach, and seems set to stay that way, your first weapon is to select the largest or most powerful kite available. Longer lines will take advantage of the wind gradient and give you the most power the kite can offer.

Check the surface of the water and the surrounding terrain. It may be that just one spot is the best, or that the wind is stronger further out from the beach. If it really is too calm, sometimes there is simply no option but to wait.

The start can be quite tricky if there is little power. The kite seems OK when you are standing on a solid surface, but as soon as you put your back foot in the board strap, you will start to drift, and hence effectively reduce the wind strength. It is quite common for riders to get their feet sorted before they begin to work the kite for power, and in the few seconds of drifting they lose control authority and the kite stalls. In shallow water you can quickly stand down again and step back as you work the kite. If you are in deep water, you are likely to lose it, and your only option is to forget the board and keep the kite aloft by work-

ing it hard; this may mean body-dragging back to the beach.

If you have practiced beach starts, this is a great time to use them as the drifting problem can be eliminated. Do remember to point a little more downwind than usual and crouch low on the board (especially as the kite turns), as this helps your balance when the pull is weakest. If you have a choice of board, choose the largest; a small wakeboard or similar can be a major handicap in light winds.

While you are sailing you can maximise power in a couple of ways. You can choose a more downwind track, or increase airspeed of the kite by working it in an aggressive pattern. If it is very marginal

The lighter the wind, the bigger the kite you need. (Photo: f8 Photography)

you may have to do both. Crouching to lower your centre of gravity closer to the board helps you stay upright in an underpowered situation. Try not to let the kite get too low as you dive it hard for power. There will be less wind lower down, as mentioned above, and as the control will be sluggish too, it is very easy to catch a wave with the kite and ditch it. A large ditched kite on a very light day can be very difficult or impossible to re-launch.

Of course you may simply not have enough wind to ride fast enough for the board to support your weight. If this occurs, you have no option but to body-drag back to shore. For this reason very light winds are quite dangerous if the breeze is offshore, as even a rider who is confident about making upwind progress can come unstuck if the wind drops. Therefore, it is important that you remain aware of the changing conditions and have a good idea of the forecast for the day. Do not be tempted by the prospect of stronger winds farther out from shore to venture a long way out to sea in marginal conditions.

Strong winds

The opposites apply! If you are still on the beach, choose a smaller kite, or if you have one select a 3 or 4-line system which can be depowered or stalled. If the kite is still overwhelming you and there is not a safe beach downwind, you may have to admit defeat and wait for the wind to drop.

If you are riding and the wind picks up you can make use of your depower loop to handle the increased force. If you are already using this or if you have a 2-line kite, you can better manage the power by taking the kite to the edge of the window.

Lofting it to the top of the window will also work, but this does mean that you will inevitably drift downwind. Once going downwind it is very hard to get the kite back down and to the side and regain directional control. The best plan is to try and control the power by brute force! Edge the board very hard and thereby create massive drag. This should give you the authority (if you have the muscles!) to allow you to get the kite to fly to the forward edge of the window and get you moving upwind. The more upwind the track, the easier it is to control the power. Try and keep the kite really low as this will also minimise the power and help you edge the board.

Gybing, particularly on a 2-line kite in this situation can be a real problem. If you do lose it you will end up following the kite downwind. This is fine if there is a friendly beach in that direction. If not, you may have to dump the kite, and may be in for a long drag while you reel it in and pack it up, followed by a long paddle!

Strong winds are no problem as long as the size of your kite matches the conditions. A smaller board may also help you stay in control more easily.

A note of caution for those using an inflatable kite on a 2-line system; a dropped kite may keep re-launching itself in strong winds and will keep dragging you downwind. It is important that you have a properly functioning release system that completely kills the kite, and that you know how to use it. If you expect to be riding in strong conditions, having a cut-away system or carrying a hook knife to escape completely if you get into real trouble is a wise investment.

Do not forget you are responsible to others as well as yourself. Riding in nuclear condition may be a risk you are prepared to take, but if there are other water users around (and windsurfers love this kind of weather) make sure you give them a wide berth. A 2 mm diameter line travelling at 30 Knots and with you on one end of it is a lethal weapon!

Kitesurfing With Others & the Rules of the Sea

Kitesurfing is a sport that takes up a lot of room! Most waterborne sports like sailing, windsurfing or even jetskiing occupy a small area of water at a time. Waterskiers and wakeboarders do of course have a line connecting them to the boat, but this is generally pretty much in line with their direction of travel. The tow boat can manoeuvre easily to avoid a collision, and of course both the boat and the skier are very familiar and very visible.

By contrast, the kitesurfer is connected by near-invisible lines to the kite that may well be at almost 90 degrees from the direction of travel. The lines are sweeping an area of the water surface up to 40 metres wide like a scythe. The kite itself is usually quite visible, though it can be obscured by a swell, but the main problem for the rider is that other water users may not associate the kite with the rider, and can

regard the space between them as clear water. Multiply this situation by 10 or 20 riders on a good day and it is easy to see how even a large bay can soon become a seriously congested place.

Riding with others. The most important rule is keep a good lookout.
(Photo: f8 Photography)

By far the most significant problem for kitesurfers is that windsurfers require very similar conditions and locations. In fact they are often the same people who simply choose their weapon according to conditions! This is good from the point of view that windsurfers will be aware of what a kitesurfer is and what they are capable of, but bad in that it means segregation is sometimes not a realistic option.

To minimise conflict there are a few common sense rulers that can help us all.

- **Try and use a separate area**, particularly when you are a beginner and will be likely to drop the kite.
- **Keep a good lookout.** This may sound obvious but holding a mental picture of the other water users that you update every few seconds by scanning the area will help you anticipate conflicts in plenty of time and either change course or hoist the kite into a safer position. It is common for inexperienced riders to look at their kite for long periods and thereby increase their risk of conflict with others.
- **Match your course and speed to other riders.** Rather than running parallel to another rider, try slotting in behind them, in this way you will be using the same sector of water as them and consequently twice as many riders can use the same area.
- **If in doubt, loft your kite.** The rider

can minimise the danger area defined by the lines by putting the kite into a more vertical position. If another rider or a windsurfer gets close, lofting the kite to quickly angle the lines upward drastically reduces the potential conflict area.

- **Take care.** If you should wipe out be aware that lines lying on the water are not easily visible and cannot be moved out of the way; so they can easily catch the fin of a windsurfer or another kiteboard. You can minimise this risk by not attempting difficult manoeuvres or using new equipment when the water is busy.

COLLISION AVOIDANCE RULES

The first thing to know about these rules is that you should never need to use them if you keep a good lookout and avoid a conflict situation arising!

● Head-on collision situation.

When two craft are on opposite courses the international convention for all watercraft is that starboard tack has priority; this means the one leading with their right shoulder has the right of way and the other craft should take avoiding action. Assuming that you are travelling pretty well cross wind for this situation to arise, your only avoidance option is to bear off downwind. *(fig 17.1)*

● Converging courses.

When two craft are converging, the one to windward (upwind) shall give way. Note the use of the word "craft": you have an equal responsibility with any other sailing craft to take action to avoid conflict. *(fig 17.2)*

Riding in company is great fun,.. as long as you all know the rules. (Photo: Advance Kites)

● Overtaking.

If you are the overtaking craft, you must make sure you have been seen and take a course that will give you plenty of room to get by without any risk of collision. If you are the craft being overtaken you must continue on your course (i.e. do not make any unexpected course changes that could increase the risk of collision)

● Jumping.

When jumping, ensure that the area you are using is clear of other water users for some distance downwind. Never try and jump physical obstacles such as boats, buoys, windsurfers or swimmers.

● Shipping channels.

If you must cross one do so in as straight a line, if possible, preferably at 90 degrees. You have no rights at all when you are in a shipping channel! Your only option is to ride defensively, keeping well away from other traffic or to avoid spending much time in shipping channels.

Always ride with consideration for others. Just because you may have a prior-

ity over another craft does not mean you should abuse this. Avoid impeding their paths where possible. (These are recreational safety rules of course; it is different in races where using your right of way to your advantage is a major tactical weapon!)

Windsurfing, sailing and many other activities are allowed in shared venues like lakes and on popular beaches, because these sports have built up a good reputation for safety and consideration. Sadly some others - jet-skiing is the prime example, are banned from many suitable locations and to a great extent it is because of the undisciplined behaviour of some of the riders.

Kitesurfers are the new kids on the block and landowners, local authorities and others will be cautious about allowing access. Asking permission, avoiding conflict with other water users and showing consideration will count heavily in our favour. We are all ambassadors of the sport!

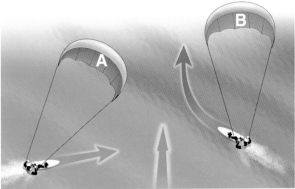

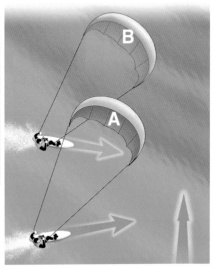

Fig 17.1: Head-on conflict, A is leading with his right shoulder and so B has to bear off downwind to give way.

Fig 17.2: Converging courses, A is upwind and must therefore give way. He could make his course more upwind or if not possible he must slow down and drop behind B.

Staying Out of Trouble & Dealing With Emergencies

Like any adventure sport kitesurfing carries some risks. These can be minimised by good care of the equipment, riding within your limits, and particularly by exercising caution with the weather conditions. However, if you keep riding long enough, an unforeseen situation will catch you out eventually.

Minor Problems

You cannot stay on the board

If you are overpowered or underpowered, or if the wind is just too gusty, at some point you will get too tired to keep trying. If you can keep the kite airborne, you will need to simply body-drag to the beach. It is vital to make this decision while you still have the energy to do this as the alternative is to ditch the kite and paddle ashore. You should be constantly aware of the balance between your available energy resources and your distance from the safety of the beach. Obviously this also varies depending on the wind and water state at any given time.

You have lost control of the kite

If you have lost control of the kite for some reason - perhaps it overpowered, is spinning or is broken in some way - you may have no option but to drop your handles or control bar and allow the safety leash to keep you in contact while the kite falls into the water. If this happens (especially in strong winds) it is impor-

tant that you wind in the lines asymmetrically (take a few metres of one side first). This will prevent the kite from re-inflating and launching while you are trying to get it under control.

Serious Problems

Unable to release the kite

The nightmare scenario is that the kite gets caught on a moving craft and the rider cannot get loose, or is blowing towards rocks. The safety leash is almost always connected with Velcro, so you should, if you have to, be able to simply rip it away from your wrist.

If you are hooked in and are unable to get the lines free of your harness hook, or have suspension lines tangled round a foot or board, then you have no option but to cut yourself free. In order to do this it is necessary to carry a bridle knife on your harness and be familiar with finding it - even underwater. These Bridle or hook knives, are perfectly safe with the blades hidden inside a narrow slot, but are very efficient at slicing through lines. They are available from good dealers or from parachuting centres. They typically cost about £10-15.

Hook knife.

Equipment failure

If you have an equipment failure, or conditions change and you find you cannot get into shore by body-dragging, you have no option but to wrap up the kite and paddle to the beach.

If you have an inflatable kite, you will need to deflate the leading edge spar(s) so that you can roll it into a loose tube. Lay this on the board and, with your upper body resting on the board and kite, start paddling. It is important that the lines are wound up and stowed cleanly before doing this as they have a nasty habit of getting wrapped around your legs. If you have a small wakeboard with minimal volume for flotation this can be a dangerous situation; if in doubt wear a flotation jacket.

One kiteboard can actually tow another if conditions are strong enough, but this may not to be of much practical use for rescue as the pulling board will be hard-pressed to make any upwind progress (probably no more than you could achieve body-dragging). However, if you are carrying a few metres of rope you may just be able to hitch a tow with a jetski or a boat.

It is important that you always know where you are. If you are riding in an unfamiliar area do not venture too far; it is easy to lose sight of landmarks if you are low in the sea with a swell.

Always ride within your abilities and with others, and if you do ride out at sea you may consider investing in some rocket flares. They are no bigger than a pack of cigarettes and can be stowed in a pocket of your harness.

If it all goes pear shaped and you do cut away from your kite or abandon your board, it is very important (and a legal requirement in the UK) that you inform the coastguard of what has happened.

Be very careful in calling a vessel to your aid as the propeller will suck in any loose line. It is important to get the lines wrapped up as far as possible before letting a boat too close. If possible signal or shout at them to approach you from up-wind with the engine stopped.

In North East England in January 2002 a kitesurfer lost his kite and it was spotted drifting by a fisherman. The ensuing air-sea rescue effort involved a lifeboat and two helicopters and cost over £38,000. The rider had just abandoned his kit and gone home. This kind of thing does not endear us to the rescue services.

If you need help the international signal for distress is to wave both arms symmetrically from the water line to above your head. If you are OK the signal is to place one hand or both hands on your head.

Beach Starting

When you are comfortable with your riding, the beach start is a useful skill to learn. It saves time, keeps you pretty dry and is much more effective in very light winds, as you can avoid drifting with your board, and the need to drag yourself out of the water.

Beach starting is simply a question of timing your initial swoop for power with stepping onto your board. It is quite easy with a larger directional, but can prove tricky with a low volume twin-tip; for obvious reasons it cannot be done when you are using bindings.

Just like a regular water start, you place your front foot on first; you then lean back against the power as you dive the kite. As you feel the force taking your weight, and driving you forward, step on board smartly. Do not worry about the rear strap immediately, as the main concern is to get the board accelerating, so your concentration should be on working the kite hard and smoothly.

Once away, simply slip your foot into the rear strap for added security.

Windsurfers will find this natural, as it is the usual system with most boards. The only problems you may find are grounding the fins if the water is too shallow, and sinking the nose on a twin-tip as the front foot may be ahead of the board's centre of gravity. In this case you may need to place the front foot behind the strap initially and adjust your stance when moving.

Beach starting is useful in onshore winds as you can get an upwind line established quickly, but if there is a strong shore break you may not have room to get going before being "waved out". If this is a problem the only real solutions are to walk around the bay to a better spot or get someone to help tow you out past the break line.

The Points of Sailing, Vectors & Apparent Wind

The Points of Sailing

Fig 20.1 represents a plan view of all the possible directions available, with you at the centre. The exact angles will vary depending on the board and kite being used and other factors. The wind is trying to push you straight downwind, but because you can vector this force (discussed below), you can actually ride on any course shown in the shaded area.

No-go zone

If you try and turn too far upwind with the kite, it will simply stop when it reaches the edge of the window, and the power will decrease. It the board is turned upwind too far it will also have too great an angle between the direction of travel and the force applied by the kite; it will slow down, come off the plane, and start to sink. The no-go zone is therefore an effective brake for you. Turn upwind and you will stop.

However, it is worth noting that the kite does not like being forced to the edge of the window, and in strong winds it is quite possible to ride, but to be unable to make the kite go the edge of the window. If you turn the board too far upwind while the kite is still well powered you will be pulled off!

Upwind beat (tack)

You can make progress upwind by tacking. The word "tacking" is used in sailing to describe two things:

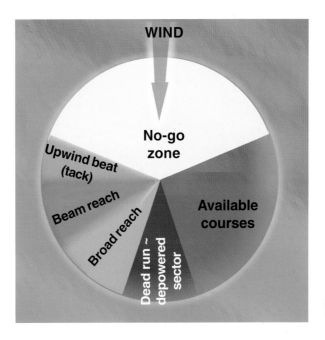

Fig 20.1: The points of sailing.

(a) the action of turning your craft by using its momentum to force the nose of the craft through the upwind no-go sector in order to change direction (not usually very practical on a kite powered craft).

(b) a course that is taking you upwind, and in this sense kitesurfers tack all the time. To ride to a point upwind of you it is necessary to sail a course as far upwind as you can, and hold each beat (course) for as far as is practical (every turn will cost you some progress). And then make a neat efficient turn and do the same the other way (*fig 20.2*).

Some kites have wider windows than others and are better at upwind courses. Some boards are also more effective than others, so the exact angle you can achieve does vary considerably. Twin-tip boards also give the facility for quick changes of direction without much downwind drift, which can be critical in making progress upwind, especially if your tacks are quite short.

It is because the no-go zone is so wide for kitesurfers that starting from a beach with a dead onshore wind can be so tricky.

Beam reach.

This simply means sailing a course roughly cross-wind. A perfect beam reach is 90 degrees to the wind, but the term is used for any more or less crosswind beat.

Because holding a beam reach track or a slightly upwind track means you are burning up a lot of your available power on drag, by edging the board, and to a lesser extent losing some power by keeping the kite near the edge of the window, this course is a lot slower than a broad reach in the same wind conditions. Kitesurfers are much slower than windsurfers in this situation.

Broad reach

This is the fastest point of sailing for kitesurfers. The board can be kept reasonably flat, minimising drag, and the kite can be worked through most of the power zone. On a broad reach a kitesurfer is pretty well the fastest thing (without an engine) on the water! Many riders will gradually work their way upwind for a few tacks, then turn onto a broad reach for a high-speed blast or two back to their start point.

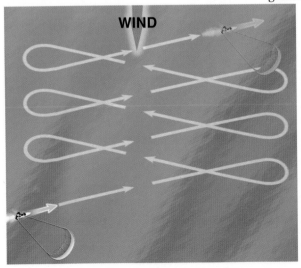

WIND

Fig 20.2: A typical tacking pattern – the scale distorted for clarity; the beats would be much longer than this in reality.

The dead-run (de-powered) zone

If you try and head dead downwind the board tends to catch up with the kite, so the power is lost and the board comes off the plane and wallows. The only way to prevent this is by adding some drag, and as soon as you turn the board to present an edge, the whole system powers up again and you are off on a broad reach.

It is perhaps possible to sink the tail of the board or progress in a series of short jumping turns, like a skier getting down a steep gully, but you can travel in the desired direction much better and faster with a few beats on a broad reach.

If you are generating plenty of drag by not being on the board at all, then the dead-run or de-power zone pretty much equates to your window for body-dragging!

Vectors

When a force, such as the wind, acting in one direction is deflected or harnessed to generate a force in a different direction, it is known as vectoring. The kite itself vectors the wind using its airfoil to fly forward, and the board vectors the force transmitted through the rider's feet to travel cross-wind or upwind. *(fig 20.3)*

A nice analogy for this is a bicycle. Ride the bike over a cliff and the force (gravity in this case) will act directly on you! Roll down a slope and the same force pulling the same way now provides a forward motion - the hill has vectored the force. Steer at an angle across the slope and it can be vectored even more, until eventually you will be going at close to 90 degrees to the original force and it will stop.

Unfortunately no-one has managed the

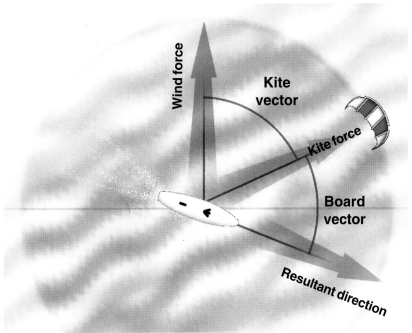

Fig 20.3: Vectors

trick of vectoring gravity so far you can travel upwards, but that is exactly what kitesurfing does with our primary force, the wind. Damn clever eh?

Apparent wind

When you are riding at some speed you will start to notice that the kite seems to be moving back away from the front edge of the window, and your course is curving downwind.

In order to prevent this you edge the board harder, which slows you down a bit and the kite flies forwards again, but as you speed up, back it goes! What you are experiencing is the phenomenon we call apparent wind.

Wind is the name we give to moving air masses, but of course it feels the same and behaves the same way if it you that is actually doing the moving.

Imagine you are in a speed boat doing say 20 knots (22 mph roughly) on a still day.

The "wind" will be 20 knots in your face; if you launched a kite it would fly behind you.

On the same boat travelling at the same speed but at 90 degrees to a "real" 20 knot wind, the apparent wind would be from midway between the true wind and the speed-through the-air of the boat; the kite now would fly at an angle behind you.

This is exactly the situation with riding a kiteboard at speed. As your board moves faster the apparent wind is coming from more ahead of you and the window moves back, taking the kite with it. Slow the board down by edging hard and creating drag and the window moves forward again. Interestingly, as your board speed increases and the apparent wind phenomenon occurs you are not only changing the wind's direction but you are also effectively increasing the windspeed, so the kite generates more power. It therefore becomes harder and harder work to edge the board at high speeds and keep an upwind course.

One way to help manage this situation is to ride with an activated de-power system to keep the kite flying fast and low near the edge of the window. When you do loft the kite and/or release the tension in the de-power loop, there is a big release of energy.

Good riders use this phenomenon to generate masses of stored energy in a radically edged board at high speed and then explosively release this power to make massive jumps.

Jumping

One of the most appealing aspects of kitesurfing is the potential for awesome jumps.

Windsurfers and waterskiers can make jumps by speeding over a ramp - usually in the form of waves or the wake of a boat - but a kite surfer can use the lift of the wing to gain serious altitude even when the surface is flat. The potential for getting airborne is what makes kitesurfing so different. And such an exiting sport to take part in and watch. It is a truly three-dimensional sport.

How do you initiate a jump?

First you need plenty of energy, so get the board travelling as fast as you can.

Unhook your harness, and sharply switch the kite direction, sending it up towards the top and rear of the window. Bend your knees, and keep edging the board hard. As you feel the power surge upwards (as the kite nears the top of the window) release the board edge and jump by straightening your legs. If you have enough power and lift, the board should clear the water. You are better off if you hit the water again moving, so bring the kite back down into the front of the window again. Whilst airborne it is much easier to control the board and pivot it into a good landing position if you bend your knees

again to bring it closer to your body.

A jump will usually result in a significant drift downwind from your original track, so after each one check you are still able to ride safely back to the beach! Jumping over people or objects is dangerous, and of course you can lose your board whilst airborne. NEVER try and jump over windsurfers, swimmers or any other person, and always make sure you have plenty of space downwind. Landing on water is fine, but landing on a beach

Photo: J8 Photography

is likely to be painful. Always allow a couple of line lengths of clear water downwind of your expected landing point.

Until you have gained considerable expertise you should remain attached to the board by your footstraps during a jump. It is important that the feet are jammed well in, as losing one strap can mean a nasty twist to the remaining leg when

Lift off .... (Photo: f8 Photography)

you land again. If you have lost a foot it is advisable to kick out the other foot as well, before you hit the water, to minimise any risk. A big directional board will be harder to control as it is relatively heavy, easily caught by the wind, and your feet will be close together and well behind the board's centre of gravity. Bending your knees and bringing it close to your body will help with control, but it can take considerable muscle power to keep it flat and pointing the right way. For this reason jumps are easier to perform on smaller lighter boards, especially twin tips or wake boards, where the feet are more symmetrically placed on the board.

Jumping is just the start.. you can do twists, loops and even change foot positions to gybe whilst in mid-air. Most riders who are into big air jumps choose to use a small board, and may execute a wide range of tricks including multiple 360's, railies (where the board is grabbed with one hand), table tops (where the board is inverted and flat above the rider), and others. Top-class wakeboarders already perform phenomenal stunts and with the additional lift and airtime afforded by a kite there is huge scope for improvisation. The sport is young and there is plenty of potential for you invent your own moves.

Just to prove the point, on the day of writing, a rider at a BKSA competition in Weymouth demonstrated true class with a jump during which he removed his "buff" (headscarf) knotted it into a pirate hat and put it back on his head before landing...

Inverted rider: note the chicken loop remains hooked in.
(Photo: f8 Photography)

Your first jumps may be made with you just hanging on to the bar, but if you are riding in strong conditions you are quite likely to be hooked into a de-power system. If this is the case you must be aware that hanging from the de-power loop will dive the kite to some extent as you are airborne. This is actually ideal if there is plenty of lift, but do ensure you remain aware of what the kite is doing as you are airborne.

Tricks and hang-time (i.e. duration of air-time) are the basis of freestyle competition. It is this potential that makes kitesurfing such an exciting and spectacular sport.

Packing, Transporting & Care of Equipment

When you have finished for the day it is pretty likely that your gear will be wet, sandy or both. Packing up a kite and lines when they are wet, and then storing them for some time can cause quite a few problems. Firstly sand. Any sand trapped inside the kite cells or simply wrapped up in the fabric can be very abrasive. It is well worth trying to fly the kite dry and then shaking off any loose sand before packing on a clean surface such as grass. Of course this is not always possible, so the next best thing is to remove as much of the sand by rinsing the kite (in fresh water if available) at the earliest opportunity. The same applies to your wetsuit, so a 20 minute washing session when you get home is generally a good idea!

If you have been riding on the sea, the salt in the water will crystallise inside the cells when they dry out. The crystals, while not as destructive as sand, can also abrade the fabric, and weaken the lines by crystallising inside the sheath in among the fibres.

Again, the best way to minimise this problem is rinsing with fresh water. Apart from the problems of wear, old water (from the sea or a lake), when left for a few days or weeks tends to smell pretty bad, so keeping your kite and wetsuit clean will also help the atmosphere in your house or car as well!

Inflatable spar kites suffer much less from sand damage, but the results of being dragged over sharp rocks or other haz-

The end of the day ...

ards can be quite serious as it is possible to puncture one of the inflatable tubes.

Drying kites is most effectively done by flying them, but if you are going to lay them out on grass or hang them up somewhere, make sure they are out of direct sunlight, or that they are packed up as soon as they are dry. The nylon or polyester fabrics that are commonly used in kite construction will only stand about a couple of hundred hours of direct exposure to UV (depending on their weight and the colour!) before they start to lose their impermeability and structural strength. This gradual deterioration is most apparent when the colours start to fade. The brightest colours such as pink and yellow will be the first to go, and fabrics in these colours can have as little as half the life expectancy of duller colours. This phenomenon is well known in the paragliding world, and is one of the reasons that kites from those manufacturers also making paragliders are rarely in fluorescent colours.

When you are not using your kite, pack it away or cover it up with something and it will last you much longer.

Lines also benefit from being stored clean and dry, and although dyneema (known as Spectra in the US) is a very strong, flexible and long-lived material, it does have a tendency to shrink when exposed to high temperatures. It is advisable not to leave kite lines uncovered in a car in direct sunlight for example.

Packing a ram-air kite is best done by laying it on its top surface. If one tip is pointed into the wind it will be much easier to manage. (If there are two of you, helping each other makes this process much simpler) You can then fold the tips to the centre (or if it is too windy, fold the kite a few panels at a time from the tip). Make sure all the suspension lines remain on the top of the kite and get folded into the fabric. Loose lines can easily get damaged in zips etc). Once folded lengthwise, gently squeeze out the air starting at the trailing edge. Valved kites may need a bit of persuasion to deflate: there is usually a velcro rip panel somewhere to let the air (and any sand or water) escape. Do not attempt to crush the air out, as this will weaken the fabric and the seams (especially when wet). When the kite is deflated, fold it from the trailing edge to the size you need for your bag or rucksack and then secure it with a strap or by putting it in the bag.

The lines can either be wrapped around the line holders provided on the bar or, if you do not have any, the best way to keep then tangle free is to "chain link" them as shown. This system makes them

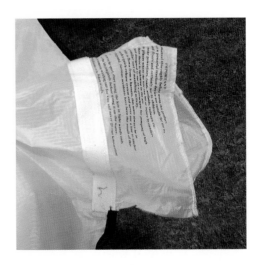

(Above) Dump Valve on trailing edge of a ram-air kite.
(Below) Chain linking lines

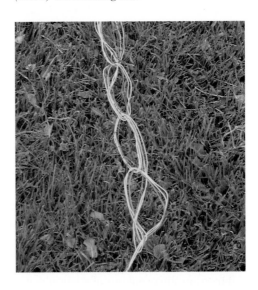

quick and easy to lay out and is much faster than winding them individually. It is well worth getting someone to show you and practising this technique.

If you have an inflatable spar kite you can deflate just the main leading edge spar and then loosely roll the rest into a long fat tube. This is very bulky but OK for short-term storage (though it does increase the risk of damage). To store it for long periods or transport it safely, it will need to be fully deflated.

Boards are extremely tough in many ways, but they are also easy to scratch or damage by knocking them on a sharp object like a small rock (or the corner of a car door!)

Always rinse off any sand sticking to your board, and if you are transporting it in a bag, try and let it dry before packing it up. (This is as much for the benefit of the bag as the board). If the board is going inside a car, make sure it cannot flop around and has nothing sharp near it. If it travels on the roof rack, get some padding around the rack bars. You can buy purpose-built pads from most watersports shops, or regular pipe lagging from a DIY store will also work perfectly.

It may seem obvious, but it is much better for the board to travel on the roof upside down so that the nose is curved down towards the windscreen and the fins are pointing upwards.

The fins (and your head) are less likely to get damaged like this as you get stuff out of the back of the car, and with many hatch-back or estate cars, the tailgate will swing up with quite a lot of force when it is opened and may hit the fins.

The nose-down position on the roof also means that the airflow at speed is pushing the board down onto the rack. If the board is tied nose up, the lifting force will be trying to rip it off as you drive and will put a lot of strain on the straps or ties holding the board down.

A padded board bag is a good idea to store

A board bag is vital for travelling.
(Photo: R. Cruickshank)

and protect your gear, and is vital if you are travelling on a plane, train, etc., where your kit will be treated as baggage. If this is the case it is obviously worth removing the fins completely and storing them in a separate bag. It also makes it much easier to carry everything, and if you need to walk a good distance from the car with your board, kite, wetsuit, towel, lunch, camera and deckchair it is invaluable!

Dealing With Damaged Equipment

Boards

If you should be unlucky enough to damage your board, then how you deal with it depends upon the material the board is constructed from. Some minor damage is possible to repair at home, but anything that fractures the outer casing of the board and reveals the foam core is going to need expert attention. A variety of different materials are used to construct boards and each need different techniques and materials to repair; the best advice is to take it to a

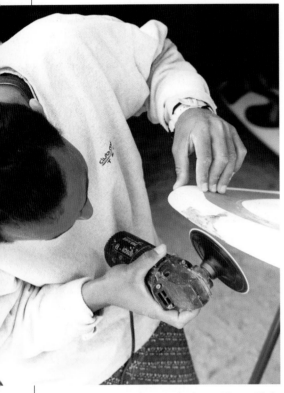

Professional board repair facilities. This is Club Mistral at Safaga, Egypt.
(Photo: R. Cruickshank)

windsurf or surf shop where an experienced member of staff can advise you.

Kites

If you have a small rip in your kite fabric (less than about 2cm), this can generally be repaired with ripstop tape. This can be found in a variety of colours at most kite dealers, windsurf shops or chandlers stores. Ripstop tape is self-adhesive and easy to apply, but do take care to round off any corners, which will prevent fraying and peeling away, and leave a good margin around the damage. It is important to lay the damaged area out flat and make

sure it is clean and dry before applying a patch. A poor job will leave stress-marks in the fabric around the repair, making it both more obvious and less effective.

A single patch on the inside of the kite is OK for very small tears (up to 1cm) and these are practically invisible. Anything larger and you will need to place another patch on the outside as well. The two patches should be of different sizes so that there is no point where the edges match. This can cause a "flex" point which will be liable to damage.

If some gentle heat is applied to these patches (a cool iron for example) then the patch becomes very effectively welded to the fabric. Sticking patches on dusty or damp fabric, on the other hand, is a short-term fix.

Blown out internal ribs or significant tears of 5 cm or more should be patched and sewn with a zig-zag stitch to make a good repair. Ram-air kites may need to be partially dismantled along the trailing edge to be able to do this, and these are jobs best done by a professional.

Inflatable spar kites are very easy to maintain in one respect, as the kite is single surfaced and easy to patch. However, a puncture in a spar can badly affect the performance and handling. Even a small puncture or leak in the main leading edge spar can render the kite unusable. The only course of action in these cases is to remove the inflatable tube from the fabric sleeve and repair it with either a drop of rubber solution glue or a patch. Glue can be used for tiny "pinprick type leaks; these will have to be located first; this is done in the time honoured fashion of immersing the tube in water and checking for bubbles. Most inflatable spar kites are supplied with glue and small patches which are very effective, although any damage greater than about 1 cm means the tube is best discarded and replaced with a new one. The same is true of any tube with a faulty valve.

When you are removing the tubes from the kite always remember to tie a piece of line to the narrow end first! (There are small velcro openings to enable you to get at the tubes to do this). Without a line to pull the repaired or replacement tube back into place you will find it next to impossible to re-assemble your kite!

Lines

A broken line when riding can be a serious problem and involve a long swim back to shore. It is therefore well worth getting into the habit of checking your lines regularly for weak spots or wear, The knots are particularly prone to damage,

and are already the weakest spots on the line, so they deserve close attention. If a broken line is repaired at sea by knotting it, it must be replaced as soon as possible as it will inevitably soon break again. A single line break may be just bad luck, but if a line breaks more than once it is safer to simply replace them both. Most experienced riders will carry a spare set of lines.

Lines should be replaced every 100 hours of riding or every year, whichever is the sooner. (You can save the old set as emergency spares!)

The harness line, or strop, that you hook into is also worth regular inspection. Because of the constant movement and pressure on this, it does wear out surprisingly quickly and if it should snap it can cause you problems.

Buying Equipment

It would be foolish to recommend specific equipment as the kites and boards are evolving so quickly. However, there are a few sensible guidelines that should help you make a decision.

As a novice you are almost totally in the hands of the dealer who supplies you, you cannot realistically evaluate kit for yourself, and even magazine reviews are far from reliable (it is a fact of life that the magazines rely on advertising for their survival and they are not going to print a review slagging off a product from a major customer).

Most riders will tell you that whatever they have got is the best thing, and anyhow, very few have actually used a wide range of kit.

That is the problem, the solution is simple, take advice from a dealer you can trust and who seems to know what they are talking about. If your first choice does not convince you then try another. Whilst some dealers and instructors are a little narrow in their outlook and tend to favour one brand they are familiar with, they are almost without exception people who genuinely love the sport and who will give you the best advice they can.

The ideal solution is to do quite a bit of kitesurfing before buying anything, but as tuition and hire is expensive this may not be a practical option.

Choice of gear and clothing depends on the conditions you are likely to be riding in. Choose a dealer who will demonstrate and let you fly the kite. Buying your first set of kit from a shop or a web site where you cannot get it out and play with it is generally a poor idea. A good dealer will give you at least an hour or two of safety training and/or set you up with a course before taking your cash!

Buying a kite

Broadly speaking, a good plan for most new riders is to buy a low aspect ratio kite that is easy to water re-launch as a first buy. These are fairly low performance, but the two problems you will be facing as a novice are handling the kite in strong conditions, and re-launching when you have fallen off. These are the areas where low aspect ratio and low performance inflatables excel.

Some closed cell ram-air kites are just about as easy to re-launch as the low-aspect inflatables, or even easier in light conditions. However, you must accept that if they do get drowned in deep water, there is no second chance, whereas you can mess about with an inflatable for half and hour and still re-launch it. Unless you are learning on an enclosed or shallow body of water, have a lot of related experience, or expect to be using the same kite for buggying or snow kiting, the recommendation is for a low aspect ratio inflatable.

The very first commercially successful kite was the Wipika Classic, and this design (though no longer in production) is still the basis for the whole family of low aspect inflatables made by a variety of manufacturers. If you start with a kite of this kind then the chances are that it will still hold a good trade in value when it is time to move on…

Deep breath… The quality of construction on many of the early models was surprisingly poor considering the price. It was quite common to spend hundreds of pounds on a kite only to discover that the manual is two photocopied sheets of paper or that the valves simply do not work. The pumps provided were often inadequate or the critical wear points were not reinforced.

Fortunately, competition is now so fierce that all the constructors are being forced to improve, but do have a close look, and always try inflating and flying the kite yourself rather than just reading the glossy adverts.

If you are buying used gear, make sure you check the kite fully pumped up and wait a while to ensure it is not leaking slowly; new bladders are easy to fit but they can be surprising hard to obtain! A customer looking for a replacement bladder for an older model from a leading manufacturer was recently told that he had to buy an entire set of six bladders as single items were not available! This will work out expensive, so make sure you check spares are available when you buy.

What size? Well the truth is you need at least two and preferably three kites to capitalise on all wind conditions, but assuming that most buyers will start with just one, I would advise a medium-to-large model as the optimum choice. For an 85kg man using a low aspect ratio inflatable, that means a kite somewhere in the 8 to 10 square metre range. (See the notes on sizing kites below) This kite will be useless in very strong winds and poor in very light winds, but should do

well enough in 14- 20 knots which is the commonest range for kitesurfing.

A lighter rider at say 65-75Kg will need to come down in size to somewhere in the 6.5-8.5m range.

These sizes are not applicable to closed cell ram air kites which are considerably more powerful.

A lot depends on the size of board you will be using, your physical strength, ability and the prevailing winds in your location. There is no substitute for good advice from your dealer.

Kite sizing

There are three basic ways of measuring a kite, flat area, projected area, and a number made up by the manufacturer!

The flat area is simply the size of floor the kite covers when laid out.

The projected area is the size of the shadow of the inflated kite (given an infinitely distant light source). Or to put in another way it is the area of kite you see when you look up at it overhead.

The projected area is a much better indicator of the power that the kite will generate and different designs may have the same flat area but quite different projected areas.

For example, a C-Quad is almost flat, and a kite with 6m^2 of fabric has a projected are of almost 6m^2. A Naish AR5 is very curved and the 13m^2 kite may project an area of (say) only 8m^2. (These are arbitrary figures for illustration only).

And it gets more complex yet! Different manufacturers use different formulae to calculate the area of their kites. At the time of writing a Cabrinha or Wipika of (say) "11.5m" is in fact about the same size as a Naish "13m" kite.

This "made up number" sizing is in not quite as illogical as it sounds. It is in fact rooted in windsurfing. In the early days, when most new kitesurfers were windsurfers who were converting, Naish (whose main business at the time was windsurf sails), allocated their kites a size that was an indicator of the size of windsurf sail that it was equivalent to. A kite that was right for a day when a 7m sail was appropriate was called a "7m" kite - even though the kite was not actually that size.

This is an unnecessarily complex situation, and hopefully all manufacturers will eventually agree on a common system.

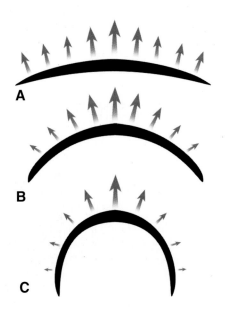

Fig 23.1:
A is a typical ram-air foil section
B is a low aspect ratio inflatable
C is a higher aspect ratio inflatable

As the sizes increase in a range the larger inflatable kites tend to be more curved, and therefore the ratio of flat to projected area becomes steadily greater. For this reason it is common for the larger kites in a range to be truly enormous in order to generate a significant increase in power over their smaller brothers. The higher the aspect ratio of the kite the more pronounced this phenomenon. A 12 m low aspect ratio kite may have a greater projected area than a 15m high aspect ratio kite!

Finally, a true airfoil section with a top and bottom surface is faster and more efficient than a single skinned foil. This type of kite is built with far less curve, and so a 10m ram-air kite is equivalent in power to an inflatable of almost twice that (flat) area.

What is really needed here is some independent body such as a magazine to (somehow!) test the actual power range of each model at a fixed line length and wind speed!

Buying a board

The next purchase is a board. This choice depends on where you will be riding; if it is on the sea then you will (usually) need to be able to cope with waves,. In this case a directional board will make it easier. If you are lucky enough to have a reliable smooth water venue, a twin tip may well be a good buy, but steer clear of wakeboards or very small boards with bindings until you have amassed quite a bit of experience.

Other stuff...

You will also need a harness; a regular windsurf seat or slalom harness will be fine. All equipment outlets will have a choice of harnesses. The latest kitesurf models have a handle on the back and a pocket to stash your hook knife; both handy features.

If you are riding in the UK or other cold climate, you will need a good wetsuit, a 5mm body with 4 or 3mm arms and legs is about right and it must fit snugly, the less water that can leak in the warmer you will be. For this reason the super stretchy material now found on many suits is a boon. Titanium neoprene is apparently somewhat warmer than the conventional material and pre-bent knees and elbows are helpful in reducing fatigue.

Thinner summer suits or shorties are only good for the warmest days, but are handy to have when you travel to warmer climes.

A lot of heat is lost through the head and a neoprene hat or cap can make a big difference when riding in cold weather. The preferred option is for a helmet, particularly where there are waves. Your board can surf around with a life of its own once you are off it, and getting whacked on the head by the nose or a fin is a painful and potentially dangerous experience.

When you are water starting, a flotation jacket of some sort does make it a bit easier as you are higher in the water, they also aid warmth and very important if you face a long swim should you be unable to re-launch your kite.

Any water start jacket or life vest must give you full freedom of movement and not have any handles or buckles that could get trapped in the lines. While larger boards act as floats, small wakeboards are little use in a self-rescue situation.

High speed and waves make a helmet an important piece of gear. (Photo: Advance Kites)

Buggies, Boards & Skis

... and other things you can pull with your kite! For hundreds of years wind power was the main form of locomotion on water. Sailing ships were the premier form of long distance transport, and they become very sophisticated and efficient vessels. Wind power never really found a niche for land transport, primarily because the terrain was too rough. The few areas where it could have been used, such as snowfields, or perhaps prairies, did not support much

traffic and in any event the horse, or sled dogs were available and much more adaptable.

In recent times we have relied on engines, and it is really only a tiny group of people who have tried to use windpower for locomotion and they have only done so for recreation with land yachts. There are thousands of people who have sailed a yacht or dinghy on water for every one who has tried it on land!

Kite Buggy with "bigfoot" wheels for soft sand. (Photo: f8 Photography)

Buggying or Parakarting

Traction kites are potentially more efficient than sails, and one of the first uses of traction kites was to power small three-wheel buggies. These machines have been around for quite a few years, and the interest in Kitesurfing has stimulated many riders to try buggying too. Many of the skills are transferable and buggies have the added advantage of being less dependent on a specific wind direction, and they allow you stay warm and dry(ish) in winter.

Learning to kite buggy is relatively easy, and because they have such low rolling resistance, they can be used with great success in winds that would be hopelessly light for kitesurfing.

A buggy typically costs around £300- 400 and are capable of 40 mph-plus on a smooth beach. They can be used on asphalt in the lightest of breezes and grass, soft sand, dirt and dunes can all be buggied given the right combination of wheels and wind!

A 4-line open cell ram-air kite of somewhere in the 2.5m to 6m range is the norm for buggying (or parakarting as many prefer to term it). The precise control of these types allows relaunching of nosed -in kites without moving from your seat, and excellent power control. You will already know that a typical water kite in sine wave mode has a powerful pull in the dive but a flat spot as you turn it back for the climb phase; parakarters can simply continue the dive into an inside turn to keep the kite's airspeed high and deliver continuous power.

But the main reason for using a 4-line kite is safety. The ground is a lot harder than water and may have obstacles like

Photo: Ozone Kites

rocks, fences and people! The ability to stall the kite and kill the power by whacking both brakes on is vital for safe operation in this environment.

Though regarded as a bit staid by some riders, parakarting can be fast and furious, with speeds of 50 mph regularly achieved. (The world record is 104 mph!)

Getting up on two wheels, 360 spins and jumps are all regular tricks, and many parakarters take part in hotly contested races. These can be simple pursuit races around a course or complex cats cradle tasks requiring navigating obstacles, tacking upwind and tactical skills

The basic skill in using a buggy lies in controlling the tension between the kite and yourself. If you steer too much toward the kite you will start to overtake it, the lines will go slack and it will stall. Turn too far upwind and you may find the kite is pulling you backwards out of the seat. Try this in a strong wind and you may find yourself having an "out of buggy experience" - think ejector seats and you will get the picture!

It is pretty simple to manage the basics of maintaining a course; most people with some kiting experience can be taught in an hour or two.

Learning to gybe is next, and again this is pretty straightforward: loft your kite and kick the front wheel hard over to turn sharply, then bring the kite back down into the new front half of the window. Making good upwind progress and following a "broad reach" downwind track requires more practice, but it is an addictive activity and every hour spent flying a kite improves your skills!

More advanced exponents may hook the harness line onto the buggy itself. This allows jumping and helps with power control, but it also means that you could find yourself being dragged down the beach in an inverted buggy with no way of releasing. For this reason, such devices are banned in most races.

The British Buggy Club (BBC) and the Parakart Association (PKA) are both national bodies that offer insurance and some guidance to members. The BBC policy DOES cover kitesurfing and at £15 per year for five million pounds worth of cover is a bargain. The Parakart association is principally concerned with racing, and offers coaching and advice as well as organising race and fun meetings at venues around the country.

Buggying is a great complement to kitesurfing, and it is growing very quickly in popularity on many of the wide sandy beaches where riders are also found.

Mountain Boards

All-terrain or mountain boards are also a growing phenomenon. Using them looks and feels very much like kitesurfing, and many riders are developing and refining their skills on these, especially when the water is cold. Using a mountain board is in fact harder than a kite board (I find!) because the steering linkage is dependent on the angle of the board. Many riders who are used to the water automatically react to the kite's pull by digging in their heels: the result is the board turns upwind and comes to a halt.

The basic technique is to steer the board by heel and toe pressure, whilst leaning back against the pull of the kite. The "toe down, lean back" position takes some practice, but once mastered the mountain board offers all the advantages of a small twin-tip on dry land, including the potential for huge airs!

Helmets and pad sets are very strongly recommended for kite powered mountain boarding - a wipe-out is likely to hurt more than at sea. If you are using your

Mountain boarding is the closest thing to kiteboarding on dry land. (Photo: Wind Designs)

mountain board on sand, it is well worth washing it down after a session as the bearings and bolts do suffer from corrosion in salty conditions.

Roller blades, 2 and 4-wheeled karts and even regular skateboards can all be powered by kites.

The golden rules are: wear plenty of padding and start with a small kite for the conditions - then work up power in small increments.

On water, kites can be used with water-skis (kite surfing in its earliest form!) and they can also be used for powering almost any small watercraft. They are particularly well suited to touring kayaks, and have been used for dinghies or even a jetski that has packed up!

The rules of dinghy sailing races are tightly defined so you cannot race with a kite; but as a parakart can often exceed the speed of a conventional land yacht in light winds - due to the extra altitude of the kite and the ability to "work it" for additional power - it is obvious that using a big kite on a sailing craft in weak conditions can make a big difference.

Snow Kiting

Snow kiting with skis, snowboards or blades is growing rapidly in popularity. Until now all these glissade sports have relied on gravity for motive power, but with a traction kite and some wind, flat snowfields, frozen lakes, and even gentle upward slopes are no obstacle. (Some manufacturers and dealers think that the potential for snow kiting is even bigger than the waterborne variety.)

Like kitesurfers, the snowboys and girls are rapidly developing the potential for big airs and tricks.

Cross-country mountain boarding! A great way to cross the wide open spaces!
(Photo: Ozone Kites)

If you fancy snow kiting then there are a few things to consider. Like buggies and all terrain boards, once away from the water (whilst it is possible to use any kite) a smaller ram-air kite is far better. True 4-line types do offer more precise control and can be stalled to kill the power if

Snowkiting on snowboards. (Photo: Advance Kites)

necessary (see previous section). A pair of wrist leashes is strongly advised too; these are simply short (1m) lengths of line connected to your brake lines and with a Velcro cuff to your wrists. As soon as you drop the kite it stalls and flutters down.

Because the wind is very often less smooth the best choice is a model with large or valved cell openings that is resistant to turbulence. Most closed-cell ram-air kites work very well for both snow kiting and kitesurfing.

Snow kiting can be done with a bar set-up like most kitesurfing, but there are considerable benefits to using quad handles like parakarting (see previous section).

You will need a harness of course; the safest bet is to use a harness with an articulating hook/pulley, i.e. one that can hinge downwards.

If you should fall over on land this will release the harness line. It may otherwise be impossible to detatch yourself from a fixed hook once you are lying on your stomach being pulled along.

Freestyle snowboards are the obvious choice of weapon as they are controlled by heel and toe pressure just like a kiteboard. And they have the advantage of being twin-tipped. Skis take a little more effort to edge as your feet are orientated fore and aft, requiring a sideways body lean to control the kite power. Fat skis have an advantage in this respect. Because they have relatively long rails, skis can be very efficient once you get the hang of them.

If using conventional skis you will need to gybe (twin-tip freestyle skis are available). Gybes are best done through a broad arc initially, keeping ground contact, but with a little practice good skiers can soon be making ariel turns.

Snow kiting schools are being set up in several places this winter (2001-2) - no doubt there will soon be instruction widely available, accelerating the growth of this branch of the sport.

The resistance offered by hard snow or ice is tiny compared to water, so a moderate wind on flat ground will probably require a ram-air kite of only around 4m or so to get blasting. Once they have amassed some experience, some riders do choose bigger kites, making them radically overpowered - the reason for this is to give lift for big jumps!

If you undertake big jumps on windward slopes, be aware that the wind deflecting upward up the hill will give additional lift. This is huge fun when you know what you are doing, but could be dangerous if you find yourself at 25m up and climbing! (We can recommend a good book on paragliding if this is your thing!)

There are also extra safety considerations in snow kiting. In resorts there will be other skiers and boarders who will (yawn) only be expecting downhill traffic. It will be a shock to them to see a couple of kite boarders ripping uphill and across the piste! Take care to give other slope users plenty of room and never cut across a busy slope. It will only take one ski school complaining to initiate a ban! Ski lifts, pylons and cables are perfectly designed to snare the unwary kite!

If you are off piste there are other hazards. You need to be careful to avoid hidden rocks and other obstacles, and if riding on virgin territory or deep snow you must be aware of hazards like tree wells, crevasses or hidden streams.

The combination of snow and wind means that losing body heat is a serious concern when snow kiting. Hypothermia is a potential killer and you should never travel far without being well equipped for the conditions. Never ride alone, and if a few of you are out always ensure the slowest person is able to keep up.

If you are riding in remote back country areas, then avalanche risk needs to be assessed. An avalanche transceiver

Snowkiting with bar and skis.
(Photo:Ozone Kites)

should be used and a mobile phone and GPS are a big advantage if you have a problem. A collapsible snow shovel is also strongly recommended. It could make the difference between sitting freezing in a strong wind or spending the night in a cosy kite-lined snowhole!

At speeds of 25mph you can cover a lot of ground and if riding in the mountains you also need to be aware of sudden dropoffs, snow cornices and sudden gusts or lulls that can be caused by the terrain. If you are riding over a frozen lake it is pretty obvious that it should have nice thick ice! (Otherwise you had better not slow down!)

Snow kiting has another element that is worth exploring: even if you go slow you will not (usually) sink. So just by adding a 3 or 4m rope you can easily tow another skier (or kids on a sledge. Do keep checking over you shoulder to make sure that you have not lost your passenger (or gained an extra couple of kids!)

Ice skates and toboggans can also be powered by kites, and treks in the Arctic or Antarctic (where kites have already been used) are obvious areas that could benefit from traction kite technology.

Competitions

Kitesurfing is a sociable sport and competitions are a great excuse to get together with other kitesurfers, ride new venues and improve your skills. For the top riders it is an opportunity to test themselves against their peers and hopefully do well enough to pick up some sponsorship.

Competitions fall into three basic levels; local jams which are mostly for the crack and social benefits; national championships, which are still pretty relaxed, but are run in a professional manner for those who are keen on making their mark; and the international competition circuit, which is an important forum for pushing back the boundaries of what is

possible, refining and demonstrating the latest equipment, and promoting the sport to a wider audience through TV and press coverage.

The kitesurf pro tour events (KPWT) are held at locations through out the world. Further information can be found at www.kite-and-fly.de.

At the time of writing most Kitesurf competitions are freestyle events - two or more riders competing head to head to do the best set, including their best moves and tricks. They are marked on difficulty and style. Specialist competitions include hang-time (longest duration of a jump) and flat-out racing.

Competition action. (Photo: F-One Kitesurfing)

Below is some of the competition data supplied by the BKSA in 2001.

Spirit of the Game

Kitesurfing is a new free sport and we ask that all competitors and officails are civil, respect-ful and polite to each other. The sport encourages Juniors and Women to enter as well as men. The BKSA does not support or encourage any attitudes that exclude anyone from this sport.

Safety and Sportmanship are Paramount

Any rider surfing dangerously or being verbally abusive will face verbal and or written warnings. Depending on the seriousness of the offence they can face disqualification from the heat, round or championship. This is at the sole discretion of the Event Organisor.

Any rider must help another rider in danger if they are capable of doing so. This will not effect the results of the rider giving help.

Competitors Basic Standard to Enter

To enter a competitor must have attained a standard of competence. A competitor must be able to launch and land (unassisted) in full control and safely in a given area. They must also be able to stay upwind in normal conditions. If a competitor does not reach this standard and is deemed to be unsafe the race Committee, race officer or head judge can order them off the water and withdraw them from the competition. They must be able to do basic jumps in control.

Each rider is personally liable for any damage to property or injury to a third party which arises out of their equipment or their actions.

There is a no protest rule in place on the British Kite Surf Championships.

The championship competition format will be Freestyle, progressed through either expres-sion sessions or single eliminator heats, depending on conditions.

There is no pre-set event programme and an information meeting will take place every day to inform riders of the programme. The event director and head judge will make the decision as to suitability of the conditions and whether the competition commences or continues.

There will be a maximum of 20 amateurs and 10 pro. riders in each round. Registration is event by event, on a 'first come' basis. Registration details will be released by the event organ-isers before each competition round.

A pro. rider is defined as anyone who is paid to kite surf or receives sponsorship, whether monetary or in equipment.

An amateur will remain so until all events in the calendar have been completed. The top amateur will move up into the pro. division in the next year, along with any amateur who now receives sponsorship.

The championship is open to British nationals only. The events may be open to non-British nationals at the event organisors discretion. A Non-British entrant will not be allowed to dis-qualify a British rider in any heat or final results.

All competitors must be members of the BKSA and be able to sign a disclaimer that they have secured their own third party liability insurance.

There are no restrictions as to the type of sponsorship promotion on a rider's equipment, even if this is in competition with the event sponsor. However, all riders must wear / display, if required promotion for the event sponsor.

Competition

Riders will be informed of specifics, alterations, or additions to these rules at the daily meeting.

The heat draws and current heat will be postioned at Race Control which will be identified at the start of the event.

A minimum of two riders will take part in each heat and judged under the following criteria:

1. *Variety of jumps - jumps on both sides, number of rotations, type of rotation, back, front, off axis. Jumps are defined by the airtime and continuing in the same direction.*

2. *Trick manoeuvres - one hand, board take-offs, handle passes, blindside, switch, grabs, the total fluidity and style of the manoeuvre.*

3. *Waves - wave riding may also be judged when waves are present.*

4. *Landing : three types.*

   a) Perfect landing when the board touches the water first, the jump / trick is 100% achieved.

   b) Water start landing when your bum touches the water and the board is sliding. The jump / trick is 75% achieved.

   c) Slam landing when the back of the rider hits the water before the board. The jump / trick is 50% achieved.

5. *The overall Style impression will be judged as 50% of the total marks.*

Riders will be informed of the number of jumps, manoeuvres or wave rides to be considered at the daily meeting. These may be changed during the day to allow for a fair competition to be judged if conditions change. Riders will be informed of any changes by a notice posted at Race Contol before their heat. It is the rider's responsibility to check with Race Control for the latest information.

Points can only be scored in the competition area, for what the judges see, not for what they think might be happening.

The rider coming in must move away from the rider coming out from the shore. If neither is going in or out, then the starboard tack rider has priority.

When overtaking kites must be raised or lowered accordingly and the upwind rider move away from the downwind.

In waves, the rider who is at the peak has priority.

Riders may not change course to hinder another rider.

All competitors must keep clear of capsized riders. No penalties will be given against a rider who collides with another rider who capsizes directly in front of them.

Riders may not enter the competition area when not competing.

Each rider will perform as an individual, but may be helped to land and launch.

All instructions issued by safety crews on water or land must be undertaken immediately.

All start times, heat durations and flag signals will be covered at the daily briefing meet.

Visual signals may be accompanied by an acoustic signal, but only the visual signals count. (See Flag and Signal Protocols at Events, below)

Each rider will compete as indicated on the heats card positioned at Race Control and shall be solely responsible for being at the right heat at the right time.

Scoring will be as follows ;

1st Pace = 20 points, 2nd place = 16 points, 3rd place = 12 points, 4th place = 10 points,

5th place = 8 points, 6th place = 6 points, 7th place = 5 points, 8th place = 4 points,

9th place = 3 points, 10th place = 2 points, Competed but not placed = 1 point

The rider with the highest amount of points, wins.

If a full Championship of Five rounds is completed, two disclaimers will be allowed. If fewer rounds are completed you will be advised as to the number of disclaimers.

If the head judge deems a competitor to be below standard or unsafe, they will not be allowed to continue.

Flag and Signal Protocols at Events

At the Race Control point the following flags are used to indicate the status of the competition. The Race Control point will be at the Judging Position unless otherwise specified.

BLACK Flag: The event is in recess due to unfavourable conditions or a safety issue.

i.e: Too little wind, too much wind, too low a tide, injury to rider, spectator, on the water etc.

RED Flag: Some Minutes before a heat this flag is raised, and then brought down 1 minute before the heat starts. The red flag also goes up at the end of a heat.

The time the flag is put up before the start of a heat must be variable depending on events of the day. It is about 5 minutes.

GREEN Flag: The Heat is on and running.

All 3 flags flying at once - Black, Red & Green

The next heat is going to start in a time specified by the Race Officier or Head Judge. Check with Race Control.

At the race control point the next heat to be run will be displayed clearly. It is the responsibility of the competitor to know which heat they are in to ensure that they are ready to start the heat when signalled.

If there has been a recess - BLACK Flag flown - it is the responsibility of the competitors in the next heat to be run to observe the race control point for the signal that the event will restart (All 3 flags flying).

To signal the end of the event for that day - all the flags are lowered.

In wakeboard competitions, individual moves like the "Elephant" "Moibus" or "Vulcan" are each weighted according to difficulty. The sport of kitesurfing is evolving fast and still making up some moves, so the competition is a little more fluid, with style an important element.

Spectators.

Paul Jobin (Chairman of the BKSA) presents the prizes. (Photo: Kiteworld Mag)

Instructor Ratings

The British Kite Surfing Association are (at the time of writing) recognising instructor qualifications from certain outside sources such as the Wipika instructor programme, or awarding qualifications to those passing a BKSA instructor course.

Passing the course is the down to the judgement of the assessor and the entry criteria to attend are as follows.

Equipment Knowledge Requirements

Kites

1. To be fully familiar with all the equipment that he/she uses for training members of the public
2. To know how to adjust and tune the equipment for varying levels of performance
3. To know when equipment needs repairing and how to have it repaired accordingly
4. To be able to select the correct kite, lines and control gear for prevailing wind and weather conditions, both for themselves and for their students
5. To fully understand all aspects of line management including knots used, line care, unwinding lines, storing lines, the danger of lines moving through the air and adrift at sea
6. To understand and be able to explain the theory of traction kite aerodynamics

Kiteboard & Other Equipment

1. To be fully familiar with all the equipment that he/she uses for training members of the public
2. To know how to adjust and tune the equipment for varying levels of performance
3. To know when equipment needs repairing

Armand, instructor at Club Mistral in Egypt. (Photo: R. Cruickshank)

and to have it repaired accordingly

4. To be able to select the correct board, fins, strops, harness, wetsuit for prevailing wind and weather conditions, both for themselves and for their students
5. To understand and be able to explain the theory of fluid and board dynamics.

Flying Skills Requirements

Land

1. To know how to launch a kite in any wind condition (aided and unaided)

2. To know how to land a kite in any wind condition (aided and unaided)

3. To be in full control (within reason) of the kite at all times 4) To know how to handle the kite in an emergency and during freak gusts

Water

1. To be able to kitesurf competently upwind, crosswind and downwind in both directions

2. To be able to kitesurf effectively and efficiently and have the ability to sail a board in reasonable conditions, putting it safely and competently anywhere.

Personal Qualities Preferred

1. Enthusiasm
2. Communication skills
3. Patience
4. Organisational skills
5. Decisiveness
6. Good judgement
7. Sense of Humour

Administration Requirements

1. To keep a detailed accident log book

2. To keep detailed records of all courses given including attendees personal information, levels of proficiency achieved, course dates, weather conditions

3. To have instructor indemnity insurance to a value of £2,000,000, third party liability.

4. To be able to supply certificates to attendees who complete the course that reflect the level of their achievement

5. To have permission from all relevant local organisations to hold kitesurfing lessons in that area

Safety Requirements

General

1. To fully understand the BKSA safety regulations (attached) and to be able to implement them along with the safety equipment specified by the BKSA for themselves and for course attendees

2. To fully understand "The Seven Common Senses".

Wind

1. To understand the power of the wind and to anticipate dangerous situations

2. To understand wind direction and how it affects Kitesurfers direction, including the dangers of off shore winds

3. To be aware that freak gusts can occur and to know how to respond to them

4. To know the difference between being under-powered and over-powered and to know what equipment to use to be correctly powered

Water

1. To know and understand that a Kitesurfer is classed as a sailing vessel and should conduct itself according to the International Rules for Preventing Collisions at Sea (IRPCS)

2. To be aware of the potential dangers of the sea, including tides, undercurrents and poor visibility

3. To assess local water hazards, such as rocks, groyns, coral, sand banks etc.

Qualifications Requirements

1. To have RYA level 2 Powerboat Certificate and preferably to add level 3 at a later stage

2. To have an officially recognised First Aid certificate

3. To have attended the relevant National Coaching Foundation course (background in coaching basics)

4. To have passed a BKSA instructor training course

The exact standards and acceptable qualifications are determined by the BKSA and course assessor, the riding standards in particular will become more exacting as demand for courses grows.

The first instructors were training using just 2 line kites and directional boards.

Now de-power systems, ram air kites and twin tip boards are entailing a much broader knowledge base for candidates.

All the knowledge and qualifications above do not make a good instructor, in order to teach well you need to have an ability to understand the needs of each student, some may be nervous and require lots of help and encouragement, some may be over-keen and need holding a back a little to perfect one element before rushing on to the next.

In many adventurous or extreme sports it is natural that people who are very competent themselves become instructors, this is a good thing, but they must also be capable of putting themselves in

the position of students who may be less naturally co-ordinated!

Teaching kitesurfing well is not an easy task, the nature of the sport means that quite a few things are happening at once, and breaking it down into easy to master portions can be challenging. Not only that, but as soon as your student begins to get the idea they are moving away from you! It requires a sharp eye for detail to see the important points they need to work on. Possibly the toughest challenge though is teaching in variable conditions or waves.

Good conditions are vital to make reasonable progress for most students. This means having the benefits of warm and shallow water and consistent winds. Getting two out of three in the UK is good going; getting all three generally means buying a plane ticket!

Get it right you idiot! (Photo: R. Cruickshank)

Having watched a number of kitesurfing instructors at work, is apparent that those that do the best job are always those who use all the range of "tools" available to them, whether it is demonstrating a skill, de-briefing clearly, or simply telling a story to illustrate an important point. If they get cold or tired pupils stop progressing and, more importantly stop enjoying the experience. So the instructors' brief includes structuring the lessons to deal with this.

Unless it has the benefit of a shallow body of water, the school will need a rescue craft of some kind, and the instructor requirements above require basic boat handling competence. (The rescue craft may well be a jetski,(of the sit-on wetbike type) which are easy to use and have the advantage of no external propeller for mangling floating lines.

Kitesurf instructors do not get rich! but there is a good deal of satisfaction from teaching people a new skill and doing something you enjoy, if you think it may be for you then try contacting your local school and if they think you have the right stuff they will help you jump through all the hoops to become a qualified instructor.

Photo: Cabrinha

The State of the Art, Innovations & the Future

The first few years of the sport has seen great progress in the standards of instruction, and the organisation of the sport in many countries, but the outstanding area of change has been in the equipment itself.

On my first attempt (in '98) the Wipika classic 2 line kite was the dominant model and there were only large directional boards or wakeboards available.

The Flexifoil boys crossed the channel with Blades (ram air open cell kites) which was phenomenal achievement, but there was no association, no proper competition circuit and no magazines!

The state of the art 1999! (The good old days)
(Photo: R. Cruickshank)

Right now we have a huge diversity of gear and things are still changing quickly, several paraglider manufacturers have joined the market bringing a wealth of related knowledge, and the snow kiting scene is just beginning to warm up (sorry).

So what of the future? It seems apparent that some of the present weaknesses of the gear will be solved by technical innovation

It may be completely wrong, but it is fun to speculate on what may happen...

A really fast, efficient kite that will water re-launch every time is the holy grail, my own view is that a fully inflated double surfaced kite that is 100% waterproof once sealed has to be the way to go, such a thing would work even after complete immersion but could be reverse launched like a ram air buggy kite. Kites with proper 4 line drag-aileron brakes are much safer too as they can be stalled and tethered to the ground safely.

Of course someone will need to invent a bar with detachable or lockable pivoting 4 line handles on it...

Kitesurfing will discover speed trials, and really fast sails based on single skin hanggliders or windsurf sail technology will revolutionise the speeds we can attain.

Boards will gradually become more specialised with speed boards, jumping boards and boards that are superb upwind, maybe these last will be convex in

Photo: f8 Photography

section with the rail in the water designed to be vertical at full speed. Small horizontal sub-surface foils might make hydroplaning practical for speed runs...

The real use of kite technology however are not directly for kitesurfing as a sport at all, but in the use of kites for larger craft. There is big money in yacht racing and even more in commercial shipping. Kites have a big future in these fields!

I asked riders from different areas of the sport what their views were...

John Thompson
(Student on a course):

"I found the practice on the beach quite easy but when you are using a board for the first time everything happens very quickly, on my course the wind kept changing in strength so we wasted a lot of time wading back to the beach and van to change kites. Because the wind was on shore if you did get going you soon ran out of room."

"The key is get the right wind in the right direction at the right place! "

"It is not an easy sport, and I expect a lot of people will be put off by these problems."

"But it is definitely cool and very appealing, I will keep on trying maybe abroad."

Trevor Sergeant
(Instructor and dealer):

Q. In your view, what is the future of kiteboarding?

A. *"New designs, materials and manufacturing techniques* means stronger, more efficient, high performance kites."*

"I believe that there is still scope to improve the overall shape and style of the kite itself, future kites will fall somewhere between the L.E.I. and the classic Ram Air Foils. A hybrid kite with small inflatable tubes with higher-pressure spars/leading edges. Water relaunchable Kites will be more aerody-

namic and more forgiving to fly. In years to come we are going to see a reversible kite no inside or outside, it will simply invert and fly, enabling superb, reliable water relaunchability."

"For now, the improvements are going to be in the control bars, as beaches become more crowded we are going to see "Reel" bars becoming popular. With the capabilities to control left or right lines independently or together. When water relaunching you will be able to reel yourself in closer to the kite giving you more control. With adjustable slip clutches allowing kite lines to spool out to full length once the kite is airborne. Perhaps even a "Beach mode" allowing dangerous gusts to actually spool out line rather than lifting the kiteboarder unexpectedly; resulting in safer kiteboarding."

"With manufacturers pushing R&D, the future is inspiring. However the real progression is going to come from smaller independents, perhaps individuals combining whole multitudes of sports into one."

Q. How did you get into Kitesurfing?

A. "Coming from a Surfboarding background. I would travel relentlessly in search of great waves. 3 years ago I was lucky enough to spend a summer season in Hossegor, France and in-between waiting for new swells to arrive. I would become bored, kicking around the beach. Suddenly the Frenchies started turning up with these kites and modified surfboards."

"All beginners, I watched with interest and amusement. Every time a kite turned up on the beach, I was there. Hassling the guys for

info. I returned to the UK and bought my first kite. Now I combine my Surfing with Kiteboarding. More time in the water keeps me happy. Pushing my personal limits, keeps me happier."

Closing words ...

In kitesurfing as a sport, I am sorry to say I expect there to be some serious accidents as more and more people get involved. Personally, I know of riders who have been dragged up a beach and hit a parked car, been blown over a 20ft cliff, hit a coral reef at speed, and gone for a sub-surface drag with a line wrapped around a foot. Every one has got away with it, but that kind of luck cannot last forever..

Almost all accidents can be avoided with good training and sensible attitude to weather and personal abilities. The way of the world is that sooner or later a student at a kitesurf school or a swimmer who gets injured by a board, will sue their instructor or the guy on the board for a million pounds for a nasty head injury or worse.

Insurance and access to public areas will become hot issues. Effective national organisations like the BKSA and, in particular, properly run local schools and clubs are the only way to ensure our sport can grow safely.

One of kitesurfings' greatest attractions is also its greatest problem. This is a fast, furious "hardcore" sport, unfortunately this also means it is difficult for weak swimmers, many children, and bluntly quite a high proportion of "Joe Public" to get into.

It is already apparent that the search for performance is more important than the search for ways to make it easy and accessible. Peter Lynn's little sit-on boat for kites or kneeboarding with a kite have never caught on, yet it is cheap and easy things like this that have the best chance of making our sport mainstream.

Maybe many riders do not want it to be a common activity, but if a million folks were buying kites and boards they would be a lot cheaper than they are now!

The competitions are already proving a hit with the satellite and cable TV companies, as they are very photogenic, if a major event makes terrestrial prime time TV then kitesurfing could get a big boost.

I suspect that snow kiting will grow very quickly, it may even outgrow kitesurfing, as the appeal of skiing or snowboarding but without having to travel to mountains (or pay for lift passes) must be pretty appealing for a lot of people.

In other sports such as paragliding, sailing or climbing there has been a bit of a divergence with racing people, freestyle people and expedition people.

Right now everything is freestyle based, but pure speed is a big attraction…

The expedition element has hardly been explored in kitesurfing, perhaps "safaris" around island chains, or coast lines, or perhaps expeditions that are part buggying, part kitesurfing or part snow kiting, will catch the publics' attention, maybe it will be you doing it? I look forward to watching the sport develop and reading the articles!

If you have any questions, answers or comments you would like to make on anything in this book or about kitesurfing, please log on to www.kitesurfUK.co.uk where, we hope, an active and useful forum for discussion will develop.

Ride safely.

Photo: Advance Kites

Useful Contacts

NATIONAL ASSOCIATIONS

British Kitesurfing Association
(BKSA)
PO Box 1580
Bath BA2 3LY

Website: **www.kitesurfing.org**   *(This website has links to many of the others listed below)*

The BKSA was set up in August '99. The aim of the organisation is to promote the safe enjoyment of the sport in the UK.

The BKSA is currently engaged in setting up a training syllabus, arranging insurance cover for members and producing news updates which are presently being distributed principally by e-mail. Instructor training, competitions and other events will be arranged by the BKSA, and it will be the main channel of communication with other national bodies.

Federation Francaise de Vol Libre
(FFVL)
4 Rue de Suisse
06000 Nice
France

Tel: 04 07 03 82 82

Website: **www.ffvl.fr**

Australian Kitesurf Association
Website: **www.aksa.com.au**

German Kitesurf Association
Website: **www.gksa.de**

Bali, Indonesia
Website: **www.geocities.com/ kitesurfbali**

Finnish Kitsurf Assocation
Website: **http.smsl.soleno.fi/surf/kite**

Italian Kitesurf Association
Website: **www.fki.it**

Greek Kitesurf Association
Website: **www.gwa.gr**

Thailand
Website: **www.cuttlebone.multmania.com**

Belgium Kitesurf Association
Website: **www.kitesurfing.be**

Hawaii Kiteboarding association.
Website: **www.hawaiikiteboardingassocation.org**

Maui Kiteboarding association
Website: **www.mauikiteboardingassocation.org**

Eastern USA kiteboarding.

Website: **www.H2air.com**

Netherlands kitesurfing association

Website: **www.http:// kitesurfen.statkabel.nl**

Switzerland

Website: **www.panicsports.com**

World Kitesurf organisation

Website: **www.kite-surf.net**

WEATHER FORECASTS/TIDES

UK weather forecasts

Websites: **www.bbc.co.uk/weather**
www.met-office.gov.uk

UK inshore waters forecast

Websites: **www.bbc.co.uk/weather/ ship_inshore.shtml**

Wendy Wind Blows. UK actual weather (coastal stations) subscription service.

Website:
www.wendywindblows.com

USA weather

Website: **www.windcall.com**

France/ European coastal weather

Website: **www.meteo.fr/marine/cote**

Tide data UK

Websites: **www.tidetimes.co.uk**
www.uktides.com

Tide data US

Websites: **www.tidesonline.com**

ON WHEELS

Mountainboards/ATB's

Website: **www.atbsports.co.uk**

Buggies/ parakarts.

Websites: **www.buggy.demon.co.uk**
www.pka-online.org.uk

SNOW

Snowkiting world tour

Website:
www.semnozkitesurfing.com

Training Information

Online kitesurf school.

Website: **www.netcom.ca/~hungvu/ kitesurfing.htm**

Flexifoil International Limited, 27 Regal Drive, Soham, Cambridgeshire, CB7 5BE, UK.
Tel: +44 (0)1353 723131 Fax: +44 (0)1353 722311 Email: info@flexifoil.co.uk Web: www.flexifoil.com

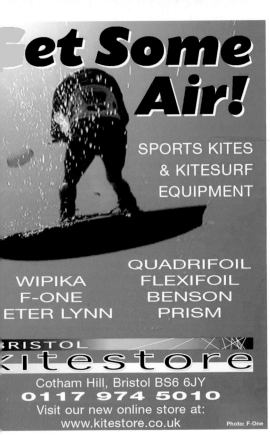

Get Some Air!

SPORTS KITES & KITESURF EQUIPMENT

WIPIKA	QUADRIFOIL
F-ONE	FLEXIFOIL
PETER LYNN	BENSON
	PRISM

BRISTOL kitestore

Cotham Hill, Bristol BS6 6JY
0117 974 5010
Visit our new online store at:
www.kitestore.co.uk

Photo: F-One

SKY SYSTEMS
kitesurfing & paragliding

tuition
sales
mail order
repairs
advice

specialists in big air technologies *since 1982*

www. skysystems .co.uk
office@skysystems.co.uk

**SKY SYSTEMS Ltd
66 Woodbourne Ave.
BRIGHTON BN1 8EJ
01273 556695**

Windtech

4/5 line High Performance Inflatable REBEL

7 / 9 / 11 / 14 / 16

- Power & Security
- 5th line option
- Manoeuvrability
- Quick-release snap shackle

2/4 Line Medium AR Inflatable

- Highest quality
- Superb performance
- Sure-fire stability
- Sweetest handling
- Super-strong construction

QUANTUM

5 / 7 / 9 / 11

Supa Strength Epoxy

WAVE'S W

GET POWERED

Christophe Roussin
French Junior Champion

Carlo Borsattino
WINDTECH & WAVES UK
KITE SURF & PARAGLIDING EQUIPMENT
info@windtech.co.uk
Tel/Fax +44 (0)1323 871383
www.windtech.co.uk

123

OZONE POWER KITES

WWW.FLYOZONE.COM

SURF - SAND - SNOW >> YOU CHOOSE

WWW.FLYOZONE.COM

> Power kites, surf boards, mountain boards, kite-bars, buggies, c-line, harnesses and more...
For more details ask at your local store or click www.wind-designs.com

sales@wind-designs.com
tel: 0870 870 6065

winddesigns
UK distributors of leisure products

Specialists for Stage2, Kheo, Peter Lynn, Windtools, Quadrafoil and Brunotti. Power kite and kite surfing specialists – call our sales line for professional, friendly service... tel: 0870 870 6065

THE BRAND NEW KITEBOARD > KITEBUGGY > POWERKITE MAGAZINE

KITEWORLD

INTERNATIONAL MAGAZINE

Kiteworld is the all-new extreme kiting magazine, delving deep inside the phenomenal sports of kiteboarding, kitebuggying and snowkiting and returning with the low down on the latest gear, hottest riders and newest places to ride. We offer a unique angle on kiting, with inspirational photography and features on those at the pioneering edges of the sport - be it snowkiting across Greenland, parakart racing at 50 mph or sailing across the Straits of Gibralter. If you're into kiting, get into Kiteworld!

DON'T MISS OUT, SUBSCRIBE TODAY!

Subscribe securely online at www.kiteworldmag.com, or call +44 (0)1273 470474

xcmedia
MasterCard VISA THAWTE

125

SIZE	17.8	16.4	11.8	10.0	8.4	6.3	4.8
DEVELOPED AERA	24.2	22.3	16.0	13.6	11.4	8.6	6.7
ASPECT RATIO	8.7	6.4	5.5	5.2	4.8	4.1	3.5

AirBlast
Leading the Revolution

The 2002 AirBlast and Switcher are again leading the charge as Wipika's total performance kite and board. The Formula One car in the Wipika stable, the AirBlast acquired subtle, but high performance refinements: more horses, tightened up the suspension, improved aerodynamics and added some rocket fuel while not changing the basic racecar. Also new, the Switcher 160 is the ultimate performance board, complementing Wipika's best seller 186 and 175. Now with new 610 fins and super comfortable straps.

A AirBlast

rider chuck patterson

Wipika®
K I T E B O A R D I N G

WWW.WIPIKAKITEBOARDING.COM
The Kitesurf Company Ltd - Distributor to UK and Ireland - Tel: 0870 8700150 - email: sales@kitesurfcompany.com

LEADING THE REVOLUTION

SIZE	15	13	11	9	7	5	4	3
DEVELOPED AREA	20.4	17.8	15.4	12.2	9.5	7.5	5.8	4.2
ASPECT RATIO	5.6	5.2	4.7	4.0	3.6	3.2	2.9	2.6

H Hydro

e Hydro and Eclipse are a new concept in eboarding for 2002. The Hydro a moderate ect 4-line kite, produces smooth power put, rock solid stability, and effortless ter relaunchability. This kite is uivalent to a showroom BMW. This e delivers high output power th smooth acceleration. The w Eclipse board, a next neration twin tip designed Jimmy Lewis, delivers the e of a wake style with ough floatation to push u through the lulls. gether the Hydro and lipse offer precise and edictable handling.

Wipika
KITEBOARDING

WWW.WIPIKAKITEBOARDING.COM

The Kitesurf Company Ltd - Distributor to UK and Ireland - Tel: 0870 8700150 - email: sales@kitesurfcompany.com

PARAVENTURE

EXTREME SPORTS

**PARAGLIDING
PARAMOTORING
PARAKARTING
KITESURFING**

**UK IMPORTER FOR
ADVANCE KITES**

For more info
On what we offer
Check out our website
Or phone us now on

01873 856009

WWW.PARAVENTURE.CO.UK

FOLLOW YOUR OWN PATH

Since 1988

NORTHERN
PARAGLIDING

Photo: Patrick Holmes

Big Thrills

on

Big

Hills

BHPA
REGISTERED
SCHOOL

Kite flyer?
GO LARGE.

Learn to
Paraglide

A full range of paragliding
courses in the Yorkshire Dales
and France with
Northern Paragliding

Call

0845 123 2555
for info

UK Courses:
www.northern-paragliding.com
France:
www.sunsoar-paragliding.com

KITE SHACK

The number one demo centre for...

- **Kitesurfing**
- **Buggying**
- **Traction kites**
- **Mountain boards**
- **Power kites**
- **Landyachts & Blokarts**

Mail Order ● Online Shop ● Part Exchanges ● Used Gear

Unit 3/4 Bridlington Experience
South Shore
Bridlington
YO15 3QN
Tel: 01262 403444
email: info@kiteshack.co.uk

www.kiteshack.co.uk

Where the action is ...

Glossary of Terms

Aerial   Any move made clear of the water.

Anemometer   An instrument for measuring windspeed.

Angle of attack   The angle between the airflow and the chord line of the aerofoil. The angle of attack determines to amount of lift produced by the kite and is variable by the use of de-power systems.

Aspect ratio   A measurement of the shape of a kite. Calculated by dividing the square of the span by the area. This figure is given in two ways: When the kite is laid out flat, or the projected area when it is flying. The first figure is of little use as a high aspect ratio kite often has a low projected (or actual) ratio.

Asymmetric (Board)   A twin-tip board with different shaped rails; only the heel-side rail is usually used as an edge.

ATB   *Abbr.* All Terrain Board (Mountain Boards).

Axel   A jump with a horizontal rotation around a vertical axis.

Batten   Stiffener in the kite, usually of fibreglass or carbon fibre, they help to maintain the kites shape. The same job is also done by inflatable ribs on many kites.

BBC   British Buggy Club. One of the UK's governing bodies for buggy users.

Bearing Away   Steering more downwind.

Beating   Making a series of tacks, each one taking you slightly upwind, so that when combined with a gybe at each end, you cover the same area of water or progress upwind.

Beaufort   Marine scale of wind strengths.

Big Air   A high jump. A big air competition is one in which the aim is to make as big jumps as possible.

Bindings   (**Full**) A boot like system fixed to the board that allows a very secure connection for the riders feet, usually found on wakeboards. (**Sandal**) A broad footstrap with an additional heel strap to hold the foot in place, usually found on smaller boards..

BKSA   British Kitesurfing Association. The UK's governing body.

Body Dragging   In-water kite control practice without a board.

Bridle lines   The lines permanently attached to the kite that help to define its shape.

Buggies (Also Parakarts) 3-wheeled land vehicles designed to be powered by traction kites. (Actually 2 and 4 wheel versions are also in use)

Carve Cutting a fast curving line through the water by digging in one edge. **Carve Gybe:** Carving a turn at speed where the board remains on the plane.

Channels Grooves in the bottom of the board to aid directional stability, usually found on wakeboards.

Chicken loop The small loop that activates a de-power system, used by hooking in the harness and allowing the bar to move away, thus transferring load from the rear lines to the front lines and lowering the angle of attack.

Cumulus (clouds) Convection clouds, cumulus are usually piled up rather than flat and indicate thermal activity and therefore variable winds.

Custom (Board) A one-off design.

De-power system Method of reducing the angle of attack and hence the pull of the kite using lines attached to the chicken loop of the control bar system.

Deck Top of the board.

Directional Board with a nose and tail that can only (normally) be ridden nose first.

Dyneema (also Spectra, Technora) Trade name for Polyetheylene line material. It is very strong and flexible making it ideal for Kite line.

Edge *(vb)* To dig the rail of the board into the water for directional control.

Epoxy Resin A common material used in the manufacture of boards.

Fakie To ride with the right foot forward (Also Goofy).

FFVL *Federation Francais de Vol Libre.* French Free-flying association. This is the governing body of Kitesurfing in France, it also governs hang-gliding, paragliding and other traction kite flying.

Foil A ram-air kite with cells.

Freeride Non-competitive riding.

Grab A move where the rider holds the edge of the board during a jump.

Gybe Method of changing a kiteboard's direction by turning the nose of the board through the downwind zone.

Inflatables Kites requiring pump-up spars and ribs to provide structure, and water re-launchability.

Knot Measurement of speed, a nautical mile per hour. Equates to 1.15 mph.

Luff When the kite becomes totally de-powered because it has travelled beyond the edge of the window. It often dives and flutters down to the water.

Manta   This is the term often used for a family of inflatable kites with a higher aspect ratio and flatter profile. Popular in France.

Mountain Board See ATB

Mutant   A twin tip board with the facility to be re-configured as a directional.

No-Foot   A trick where the board is taken off the feet in mid air. (Some boards now have a handle for performing this!)

Off the Lip A turn made on the crest of a breaker.

Offshore   (Wind) When the wind blows from the land to the sea, sometimes known as a 'land breeze'.

Over Powered   When the kite or wind is too much for the rider to handle.

Paragliding   A form of free flight using a ram-air canopy.

PKA   Parakart association, like the BBC but the PKA concentrates primarily on race meets.

Power band   The sector of the window where the kite is producing significant power.

Pro Tour   International competition circuit.

Ram-Air Kite   Double surface kite design relying on movement through the air to maintain its inflated aerodynamic profile.

Ribs   Inflatable kites: the inflated tubes running fore-aft giving shape to the kite. Ram-air kites: the vertical panels of material separating the individual cells of the kite.

Rocker   The curvature of the underside of the board. Nose rocker is known as the scoop, tail rocker as the lift.

Rogallo Kites   Single surface kites using rigid tubes for support. Named after the inventor Francis Rogallo.

Sea Breeze Phenomenon of an onshore wind picking up on warm days.

Shore Break   The line of surf where the waves break as they approach the beach.

Skimboards   Small finless boards that occasionally been powered by kites. They will work in as little as a centimetre of water, but they cannot be ridden upwind.

Snow Kiting   Any traction kiting on snow. Skis, sleds and snowboards all work well.

Stall When the angle of attack of the aerofoil becomes too high, the airflow breaks away, lift is lost and the kite falls backwards.

Thermal   Bubble or column of rising air.

Traction Kite   Powerful kite used for pulling a kiteboard, buggy or similar.

Toe Down Riding with the toe edge of the board gripping the water, also known as forward-side.

Twin Tips   Boards that can be ridden in either direction without turning.

Wakeboard   Small type of board used with bindings for water skiing, and now kitesurfing

Wind Gradient   Reduction of windspeed near the surface due to friction.

Window   The available kite positions for a given combination of kite and conditions.

Windward   Upwind, the direction looking into the wind.

Zenith   The highest point above the rider's horizon attained by the kite.

Index

Wind Strength Conversion Table

Force	mph	Knots	kph	m/sec	Description	Sea State	Land Indicators
0	<1	<1	<1	0 to 0.2	Calm	Smooth	Calm. Smoke rises vertically
1	1 to 3	1 to 3	1 to 5	0.3 to 1.5	Light Air	Ripples, no appearance of scales. No foam crests	Smoke drift shows direction Vanes do not move
2	4 to 7	4 to 6	6 to 11	1.6 to 3.3	Light Breeze	Small wavelets, smooth crests.	Wind felt on face, leaves rustle Vanes move
3	8 to 12	7 to 10	12 to19	3.4 to 5.4	Gentle Wind	Large wavelets, crests begin to break. **Kitesurfing becomes possible**	Leaves and small twigs move light flags extend
4	13 to 18	11 to 16	20 to 29	5.5 to 7.9	Moderate Wind	Waves up to 4ft may form, whitecaps evident. **Good conditions.**	Leaves and rubbish blows around, flags flap, small branches move
5	19 to 24	17 to 21	30 to 38	8.0 to 10.7	Fresh Wind	Waves up to 8ft m, many whitecaps, some spray. **Ripping conditions**	Small trees start to sway, flags ripple
6	25 to 31	22 to 27	39 to 50	10.8 to13.8	Strong Wind	Waves up to 13ft , foaming whitecaps, spray. **Skill & small kite required!**	Large branches sway, whistling in wires may be heard.
7	32 to 38	28 to 33	51 to 61	13.9 to 17.1	Near Gale	Waves up to 20ft, white foam blown in streaks. **Go Home**	Whole trees in motion, felt resistance when walking
8	39 to 46	34 to 40	62 to 74	17.2 to 20.7	Gale	Waves up to 20ft. Edges of crests break. Dense foam streaks. **Stay at home**	Trees in motion, strong resistance to walking.
9	47 to 54	41 to 27	75 to 86	20.8 to 24.4	Strong Gale	Rolling seas, waves, foam and spray are evident. **Stay in bed**	Slight structural damage occurs.